THE 250 PERSONAL FINANCE QUESTIONS

for

Single Mothers

SUSAN REYNOLDS AND
ROBERT BEXTON, CFA

BUSINESS

Avon, Massachusetts

Published by Adams Business, an imprint of Adams Media,
a division of F+W Media, Inc.
57 Littlefield Street, Avon, MA 02322. U.S.A.
www.adamsmedia.com

ISBN 10: 1-59869-965-2
ISBN 13: 978-1-59869-965-4

Printed in the United States of America.

J I H G F E D C B A

Library of Congress Cataloging-in-Publication Data
is available from the publisher.

Contains material adapted and abridged from *The Everything® Guide to Personal
Finance for Single Mothers*, by Susan Reynolds and Robert Bexton, copyright © 2007
by F+W Media, Inc., ISBN 10: 1-59869-248-8, ISBN 13: 978-1-59869-248-8.

This publication is designed to provide accurate and authoritative information
with regard to the subject matter covered. It is sold with the understanding
that the publisher is not engaged in rendering legal, accounting, or other professional advice. If legal advice or other expert assistance is required, the services of a competent professional person should be sought.
—From a *Declaration of Principles* jointly adopted by a Committee of the
American Bar Association and a Committee of Publishers and Associations

Many of the designations used by manufacturers and sellers to distinguish
their products are claimed as trademarks. Where those designations appear in
this book and Adams Media was aware of a trademark claim, the designations
have been printed with initial capital letters.

This book is available at quantity discounts for bulk purchases.
For information, call 1-800-289-0963.

DEDICATION

This book is dedicated to all single mothers who are working diligently to create a brighter future for themselves and their children—you can do it, ladies!

ACKNOWLEDGMENTS

We wish to thank Adams Media for its quest to provide substantial, yet easy-to-understand, financial books that genuinely help women improve their finances. In particular, we'd like to thank Chelsea King, Paula Munier, and Lisa Laing for the opportunity to provide this helpful guide.

CONTENTS

INTRODUCTION

Like it or not, a divorced, widowed, or a not-yet married or never-married mother is a woman on her own—a woman forced to take responsibility for every aspect of her newly single life (kids or no kids). A divorced, widowed, or unpartnered mother has to deal with financial realities and make financial decisions that will affect herself and her children for decades. An informed single woman must, indeed, develop the skills and the confidence to make smart decisions and gain control over her financial reality.

Divorce is a financial disaster for most families and for the economy. Almost half of all divorced fathers fail to make their child-support payments. Only 25 percent of divorced fathers pay full child support, but even then it is far more likely that the divorced mother's—along with the children's—income has decreased substantially. Average visitation for divorced fathers is around once a month, and divorced women with minor children make up a major segment of Americans living below the poverty line. In addition, single mothers often sacrifice their own welfare—including financial—for the sake of their children.

This book has been researched and written to steer you through whatever personal financial minefields you are navigating and to help you build an operational vocabulary that will give you a real leg up on handling your personal finances. It is designed to be an invaluable resource as you find your way through the money jungle. As your family and finances grow and as you meet critical financial turning points in life, like the purchase of a home or helping your child pay for his or her college education, the advice in this book will guide you. If you apply this information to your finances, you will be on the way to achieving your financial goals and claiming financial independence, one step at a time.

Chapter **1**

ON YOUR OWN ... AGAIN

WHILE THERE CAN BE MANY, many benefits to being single, being a single mother presents an enormous challenge. Even if you came out of the death, divorce, or separation with a safe cushion of money and assets, you will now be fully responsible for all the financial decisions that will directly affect you and your children for decades to come. If you are not money-savvy, this could cause massive anxiety or lead to impulsive decisions that undermine your long-term security. It's time to gather yourself and begin again.

Question 1: **What do I do if my husband suddenly dies or files for divorce?**

First, you have to accept that absolutely everything has changed. You cannot go forward with a solid base if you don't get a firm grip on what your situation is now and from this point forward. You have to think for yourself, and think smart. The first precept might simply be "do no harm." If you are uncertain what to do, keep the status quo until you feel more confident about your course of action. Focus on what requires your immediate attention: paying down debt or creating an emergency fund, for example. The first—and very important—task is to discover and record all aspects of your financial situation, as follows:

- Create a list of all your income.
- Create a list of all credit card and loan balances.
- Create a list of all retirement and savings accounts.
- Create a thorough list of all monthly expenditures.
- Create a temporary livable budget that reflects your new circumstances.
- List and review insurance policies.
- If needed, name your children as beneficiaries on insurance policies, CDs, bank accounts, and retirement plans.
- Select guardians for your children.
- Create a rudimentary will and a living will until you can more properly create a lasting one.

Other than fulfilling the necessary, immediate tasks—establishing how much money you really have to live on, how it will be dispensed, and what you have to work with—it's advisable to wait at least six to twelve months before making major or long-term decisions related to money. Even if you feel pressured, allow yourself time to steady your emotions and learn as much as you can about financial management before making major changes.

Question 2: **How do I make long-term, calculated decisions?**

After the dust has settled and your grief is subsiding, it's time to contemplate your long-term goals and to make decisions that will help you accomplish them. Sit yourself down and make a list of things you want to create for the future and what you need to address now to make them happen. Examples include the following:

- Can you afford to stay in your current home?
- If not, where do you want to live? What can you afford?
- How can you move up at work or increase your income?
- What are your long-term financial goals, and how do you plan to achieve them?

- Do you need, or desire, additional education?
- How will you fund college or additional training for yourself or your children?
- How will you increase your savings and fund a retirement plan?

What you're seeking are generic ideas about what you want to create for the future and whether you need to weigh them in making decisions that deal with your immediate, pressing needs.

Some immediate tasks that you need to undertake are:

- Create a household inventory for insurance purposes.
- Copy and store important documents.
- Set up a system to manage bills.
- Balance your checkbook monthly.
- Check all credit card statements to make sure the charges belong to you, and match up corresponding receipts.
- File deductible receipts in a tax file, and file warranty receipts in a warranty file.
- Check tax returns, and establish a file for each of the last five years.

Question 3: **What's the best way to get organized?**

Select a drawer, a file holder, or a basket in which to store monthly bills. Open all mail when it arrives. Discard junk mail, and immediately shred all those endless credit card offers. Then, put all your bills into the designated, easily accessible drawer, file, or basket. Create a monthly payment schedule to remind you when bills are due. You can opt to have most bills arrive the first of the month, the middle of the month, or the end of the month. If you have sufficient money in your checking account, pay bills when they arrive. Alternately, set up automatic payments from your checking account, or select at least two days a month when you pay bills.

It's prudent to buy and use an accounting program, which are very easy to use and helpful in simplifying and expediting your bill paying.

Question 4: **Speaking of averting disaster, how do I hold my ex-husband accountable?**

According to the government, more than half—half!—of all fathers who owe child support do not pay it. The Child Support Recovery Act of 1992 enacted laws that make it a federal crime for fathers to default on court-ordered child support due children living in another state. Your local child support enforcement office can assist you in taking measures to force payment. (You can also find help online, at *www.singleparentcentral.com*.) If you report the father's failure to pay to the IRS, for example, they will divert any refunds he earns to you.

If your former husband or partner fails to pay child support, it is imperative that you act immediately by filing a motion for contempt of court. Although it's wise to use an attorney, this is something you can file and present to a judge. But don't wait, because it will take weeks before you have a court date. On that date, the alleged violator must appear in court to explain why he has not complied and why he should not be held in contempt. If the person is found guilty of contempt, the judge can seize his assets, levy fines, and even send him to jail.

Question 5: **How do I track down a deadbeat dad?**

As of 1998, federal law requires employers to turn in the names, addresses, dates of birth, and Social Security numbers of all new hires, which means that even if the father has crossed a state line, it's easier to find him today than it was in the past. Some of your options for tracking down a deadbeat dad include searching these areas:

- Motor vehicle records
- County tax records
- The IRS
- Social workers

Although it can be difficult and frustrating, holding the father financially accountable is important to your children's future.

Question 6: **How do I handle finances if I hook up with a new man?**

If you're at the move-in stage, ask for a meeting at which you will share credit reports, FICO scores, credit card and loan balances, and net worth statements. This will be your opportunity to find out his true situation and to find out how he handles his financial responsibilities. It would also be a good idea to ask to see the last three years of income tax reports, as well as records of child or spousal support and payroll stubs. You are entitled to know the absolute truth about his financial situation.

Question 7: **Should we keep our finances separate?**

In the beginning, particularly if you aren't buying a house together or otherwise mingling debt, it makes sense to keep the majority of your finances separate. You can establish a common household account, and then as the relationship grows, you can begin to merge your financial assets and debt. It's always wise to have some money that remains yours to control, whether it's a clothing budget or mad money.

It's also important to discuss behavioral expectations. If you want to sit down together every month to pay joint expenses, balance the checkbooks, and create new goals, make sure he understands how important this is to you. If you agree to turn everything over to him but are uncomfortable not being on top of things, ask for a monthly meeting in which you review all the finances. Maybe you want joint meetings before any major purchases, or you'd like to establish joint savings that build toward the purchase of a new car. Whatever you require to make you feel secure, knowledgeable, and powerful within the relationship is, and will remain, important. It's the failure to talk about finances clearly that creates problems that can quickly become—or at least feel—insurmountable.

Question 8: **Should we find a way to make it official?**

Absolutely! Instead of counting on your romantic feelings to pacify all problems, take the time to write out a very concrete "cohabitation agreement" that will specify the financial agreement you have worked out together—your mutual rights and obligations with respect to joint and separate property from now on. Define both partners' expectations and how they will be met, or worked toward. Without a written cohabitation agreement, it will be difficult to exercise your right to receive support, share in assets acquired during the length of the relationship, make medical decisions on his behalf, or claim an inheritance.

Question 9: **What if he moves into my house?**

Your house is most likely your most valuable asset. As such, it's not wise to rush into co-ownership of houses, so if he is moving into your house, you may want him to pay rent for a period of one year, at which time you will renegotiate. If you decide to purchase property together, consult a lawyer or financial consultant to determine the best way to structure ownership. "Joint tenant" means that the survivor owns the property in event of the other's death, while "tenants in common" means that the property goes to the deceased's estate, so that heirs end up owning the property. If you're paying down 60 percent to his 40 percent on a new house, state that clearly, and specify how you want that to be handled in the event of a sale.

Question 10: **What about my other assets?**

Of course you will also want to protect your assets. Make a list of everything you own, including investments, furniture, and heirlooms. Co-ownership from the point of cohabitation can be negotiated, but what's yours prior to the relationship should remain yours. Also, to fully protect your children, leave them listed as your beneficiaries on bank accounts, insurance policies, investments, or wills. If you decide to marry, by all means renegotiate the financial agreement, keeping in mind that once you marry, each person will become mutually responsible for both parties' financial management.

Chapter **2**

WHERE YOU WANT TO BE: SETTING GOALS

CREATING PERSONAL FINANCIAL goals is extremely important and worthy of your complete attention. James Cash, the founder of J. C. Penney, said it in a more succinct and poster-worthy way (as in, paste it onto your bathroom mirror so you can live it as a credo): "Give me a stock clerk with a goal, and I'll give you a woman who will make history. Give me a woman with no goals, and I'll give you a stock clerk."

Question 11: **What's the single most important thing I need to do?**

Establishing, and then living up to, a set of goals that will propel you forward and create financial health. Creating goals is a means to an end. Goals provide a roadmap. They give you a point on the horizon to focus on and then help you harness the energy to get there step by step. Long-term goals are really the formulation and clear statement of your dreams—what you want to accomplish in your lifetime. Short-term goals are the blueprint for achieving those dreams. Only by illuminating the stepping-stones along the path are you able to take potent steps that lead you forward.

Pablo Picasso, one of the greatest and most productive artists of all time, believed in goals and stated so clearly: "Our goals can only be reached through a vehicle of a plan, in which we must fervently believe, and upon which we must vigorously act. There is no other route to success."

Question 12: **How do financial goals serve me on a daily basis?**

Goals help you every day by helping you come closer to fulfilling your dreams. In fact, the first step is to contemplate what is most important to you and to establish a list of values. Values are your spiritual bottom line—what will ultimately bring you meaningful pleasure. Of course you value your children, but what is your intention toward them? Perhaps it's building a secure future, which could entail establishing educational funds and providing a stable home in a safe neighborhood. Perhaps it's having more time to spend with them while they are young, or creating a business that will support all of you for the next ten years and build resources for your retirement, so you won't be a burden on them.

Question 13: **What should be my first and single most important goal?**

The absolute first thing you need to set your sights on is creating an emergency fund. Every financial advisor/writer in the world stresses this point, and every struggling woman moans. Of course it's hard to accumulate a single month's expenses—let alone the recommended three—to cover emergencies. It's the reason insurance was invented, but emergencies arise that are beyond insurance. Cars break down, children break legs (requiring a babysitter while they recover), roofs leak, hot-water tanks fizzle, landscaping fries, and sometimes a woman needs a break.

Fat emergency-fund accounts accumulate interest and allow you to sleep soundly. Make your first short-term goal to be opening an emergency savings account of at least two month's salary. This cash pillow is requisite before you make any big purchases or start investing.

Question 14: **How do I create long-term goals?**

Long-term goals often require you to work toward them by fulfilling a series of short-term goals over a long period of time. The long-term goals are really your dreams—the circumstances you want to create that will bring you inner happiness—but they require a belief that you'll get there eventually. They also require an ability to sustain belief and expend energy.

To create these kinds of goals, you need to look deeper than the task at hand. If your heart's desire is to build a foundation of security for yourself and your children, that's a laudable and valid lifetime goal, but you will need to break it down into a series of achievable goals. Long-term goals might include buying a home in three to five years; saving $30,000 over the next ten years; paying off your mortgage in twenty-two, rather than thirty years.

Once you define what you want, why you want it, when you want it, and how to get it, write specific, measurable, and achievable goals. Create target dates and a list of tasks required. Then place a list of your goals in prominent places—your bedroom, your home office, and your refrigerator—so that the daily reminder will spur you on to success.

Question 15: **How do I create short-term goals?**

Short-term goals break down your long-term goals into manageable bites. Each time you achieve a short-term goal, you are moving closer to the ultimate, long-term goal behind it. Some believe in doing something daily that works toward fulfillment of your short-term, manageable goals. As long as you create them and set a viable deadline for achieving them, you're on the right track. Short-term goals should be all of the following:

- **Specific:** You should be able to state the goal in positive language and break it down to its smallest denominator.
- **Measurable:** The goal should provide quantifiable, visible results within a certain time frame.
- **Attainable:** Attaining the goal should be a bit of stretch, but definitely within your reach.
- **Valuable:** Achieving this end should align with your core values.
- **Progressive:** Achieving this goal should also be a step toward a long-term goal.
- **Primary:** Your identified goal should be a top priority that will motivate you to get going.

Question 16: **How do short-term goals differ from tasks?**

People often confuse short-term goals with tasks, and it's important to distinguish between them. Tasks are a series of to-do items that you need to address to move you closer to achieving a short-term goal. A short-term goal is a bar you set for yourself that achieves something of value. If your short-term goal is to get your finances organized, you could break it down into the following tasks:

1. Buy filing folders.
2. Separate all your bills, bank statements, loan statements, investment statements, tax returns, and so on.
3. File the physical copies in clearly marked folders.
4. Research and buy a financial and budget tracking software program.
5. Enter all the pertinent data that will allow you to stay on top of your monthly finances.

Question 17: **How do I decide which goals take priority?**

If you have massive credit card debt, or delinquent accounts, addressing these crisis situations needs to be a top priority. The cost of carrying high-interest debt or allowing delinquencies to affect your FICO score will defeat goals before you get them off the ground. Once you've fought the debt dragon, you can refocus your goals on savings and wealth creation.

Question 18: **How do I increase my chances of meeting my goals?**

Accentuate the positive. The whole point of making goals is that you are creating a positive vision of your future. If goals are conceived as punishment, you won't feel inspired to achieve them. Instead of writing, "I won't spend any money on luxuries for six months," write "I am choosing to pay down my credit card debt to zero." It's not deprivation; it's empowerment!

Question 19: **How often should I review my progress?**

It's advisable to review your progress toward short-term goals at least every three months. Some questions to ask include the following:

- Are your short-term goals effectively working toward your long-term goals? If not, what needs to be changed?
- Are you making the returns on your investments that you need to meet your long-term goals? If returns have been falling short, you either need to save more, or find a higher-return investment to meet your goals.
- What caused the missteps? Did you miss your savings hurdle because of unexpected one-time expenses, or because you fell off the budget wagon? What do you need to do to get back on course?

Question 20: **Why is the frequency of review important?**

Reviewing your goals every three months means that your assessments will allow you to make any adjustments to existing goals—extending or shortening the completion date, adjusting the tasks, raising or lowering the financial reach, or whatever is required—and get back on course quickly. If your long-terms goals still reflect the dreams you want to manifest, and you have reached some, or all, of your short-term goals, you can create a new set of logically ordered, short-term goals that will maintain the momentum.

Chapter 3

TAKING CONTROL OF YOUR IMMEDIATE FINANCES

EXPERTS ESTIMATE THAT some 42 million Americans live paycheck to paycheck. In surveys, 60 percent of Americans revealed that a one-week delay in receiving their paycheck would result in failure to pay an essential bill, such as mortgage, rent, or car payments. If you're similarly living on the edge, it's time to pare back expenses or generate more income. In other words, it's time to take control of your finances!

Question 21: **What is the first thing I need to do to take control of my finances?**

One of the first things you need to do to gain control over your own finances is an honest assessment of your current financial flows. Every single mother needs to know how much money is coming in, how much money is going out, and how much she owes to credit card companies, banks, or other creditors. You cannot build a financial future without a clear picture of what you owe, what you earn, and where your money is going.

Question 22: **How detailed do I have to be when tracking expenses?**

It's important to figure out every conceivable expense that weighs down your true-life spending pattern. Use the following list as a guideline for creating the in-depth list of expenses you will need to create a thorough, realistic, functional budget:

- Rent or mortgage
- Personal and residential taxes
- Medical insurance, dental insurance, glasses or contact lenses, medicine, co-pays
- Car insurance, gas and car maintenance, parking expenses, tolls
- Home or renter's insurance
- Utilities (electricity, water, gas), Internet, cable, phone
- Groceries, eating out, entertaining at home
- Loans or credit card payments
- Savings
- Tuition or student loans
- Grooming expenses (haircuts, cosmetics)
- Clothing and clothing maintenance, shoes, coats
- Entertainment (movies, concerts, book purchases, coffee, night out with the girls)
- Special occasions (birthdays, weddings, Christmas)
- Emergencies
- Professional associations, conferences, classes
- Gym or club memberships
- Vacations, getaways
- Veterinary bills
- Children (school activities, tuition, child care, medicine)

Question 23: **What would a realistic budget look like?**

Here's a sample budget reflecting narrow margins and a budget that restrains spending; i.e., a budget for someone making tough choices to live within her means:

Sample Budget for One Month

Income	
Salaries, wages, tips, etc., as well as interest on checking account, after taxes	$3,000
Savings	
Savings to build two-to-five month emergency cash balance	$50
Savings for down payment	$100
Savings for retirement	$150
Savings for children's education	$10
Savings for vacations	$50
Savings subtotal	$360
Required expenses	
Mortgage or rent payment, including homeowner's or renter's insurance	$850
Utilities—electric, garbage, water, heat	$80
Food, excluding fancy nights out and alcohol	$550
Medical and other insurance premiums	$30
Clothing, including cleaning	$100
Car payments, insurance, maintenance, public transit	$300
Telephone and Internet	$45
Credit card and other debt	$25
Child care	$100
Other required expenses	$250
Required expenses subtotal	$2,330
Expendable expenses	
Food eaten out, alcohol, other nonrequired food expenses	$40
Movie rentals and theater visits, including snacks	$15
Vacation expenses	$40
Cable and nonessential Internet and telephone	$50
Gifts and donations	$10
Other expendable expenses	$50
Expendable expenses subtotal	$205
Subtract savings and all expenses from income; this is your budget buffer	$105

If you can manage it, it's very wise to save the amount of your budget buffer. If your buffer figure is negative, you need to cut expenses and/or increase your income.

Question 24: **How often do I need to review my budget?**

Review your budget regularly (once a month is ideal) and make adjustments to reflect changes. If you have fallen short for two straight months, write down every cent you spend and track the source of excess. Sticking your head in the sand will only make the situation worse. Get the matter in hand and trim where necessary. You'll feel better and get back on top sooner.

If your salary bumps up slightly, make sure you know exactly how much extra cash is actually coming in before you rush out to buy a fancier car, allocate a healthy portion to paying down your credit card debt, or up your monthly savings.

Question 25: **Once I have a workable budget, what's the next step to financial health?**

Your next task is to calculate your net worth. Your net worth is the total value of your liquid assets minus your debts. Assets include cash, stock, bonds; the equity in your home; and any personal property you could sell relatively fast, like extra cars or jewelry. Debts include car loans, mortgages, home equity loans, furniture loans, student loans, and credit card debt.

Planning your financial life without knowing your net worth is like trying to navigate a remote, unknown territory with a map but no idea of where you are on the map. You might take purposeful steps in one direction, but if you don't know where you are, you won't end up where you want to be.

Calculating your net worth shows you exactly where you stand financially.

Question 26: **How do I value my assets?**

You might automatically put your car down as a valuable asset, but unless you're in the process of selling the car and won't buy a replacement, you'll never see that value as cash. A car is a depreciating asset. The same can be said for jewelry and other personal property that you aren't in the process of selling. Even if you could part with valuable jewelry, you would probably only achieve 50 to 80 percent of its retail value. Some financial advisors include the cash value of life insurance policies in the assets column, but unless you are in the process of redeeming them for cash, they may skew your net worth calculation.

Question 27: **How would a worksheet reflecting my net worth look?**

Create a two-column worksheet, as the sample below illustrates, and then record the value of your assets in one column and the amount of your liabilities, or debt, in the other. Subtract your liabilities from your assets to determine your net worth.

Calculating Your Net Worth

Assets (add)	Liabilities (subtract)
Home (appraised value)	Mortgage
Car	Loan balance
Jewelry	Equity loan
Antiques	Credit card balances
Bonds	Student loans
Total assets	Total liabilities
Net worth = total assets minus total liabilities	

Once you have a clear picture of what you really have, and what you really owe, you will see where improvements need to happen.

Question 28: **When should I consult a financial advisor?**

After you have computed your net worth, established a budget, and outlined your debts and devised a plan to conquer them, it's time to sit down with a financial advisor. This professional can help you better understand your true situation, refine your goals, and advise you how to best invest whatever money you do have.

To find a financial advisor, ask around among friends and coworkers, call your Better Business Bureau, or ask your banker for references. Once you've selected three potential advisors, ask them if they are willing to meet with you briefly to see if they are the right fit for you. You may be able to assess this over the telephone, but it's always helpful to see the person before you make a final decision.

Question 29: **What should I ask the financial advisor?**

One of the first things you want to ask is how they are paid. Many financial advisors are paid on commission, which means they receive large payments for selling load mutual funds, annuities, or other investments to you. There is an obvious conflict of interest when you deal with financial advisors who profit by generating activity in your portfolio that may leave you less well off financially. If you have enough money, use a fee-only financial advisor, who may have a professional designation like CFP or CFA after his or her name. Fee-only financial advisors are paid based on the amount of assets they manage, so the more money they make for you, the better off they are. As a result, fee-only advisors are more likely to work for your benefit when considering investments.

Question 30: **What would be a reasonable fee range for a financial advisor?**

Many fee-only advisors charge fees for advice—from a couple hundred dollars for a financial plan to thousands of dollars for a family financial plan including estate work (wealth transfer to kids and grandkids, accounts used to minimize taxes, and related legal and tax consultation). Most fee-only financial advisors also charge 0.75 percent to 1.5 percent of assets per year. Often, you can get free or lower-cost financial advice through discount brokers like Charles Schwab, particularly if you are a client.

Question 31: **How should I prepare to meet with a financial advisor?**

Pull together a financial plan that you think could work. Also consider the risk you are willing to take and all the large expenses that you need to make over your lifetime (paying for your children's education, buying a home, taking care of your parents in their old age, and so on). Your advisor will appreciate that you are prepared, especially if you arrive with an open mind, ready to listen to and take the advisor's suggestions.

Question 32: **How do I evaluate a financial advisor?**

The National Association of Personal Financial Advisers (online at *www.napf.org*) provides a financial advisor checklist that will help you determine whether you've found the right advisor for your needs. Check out the site to see if yours adds up!

Question 33: **Do I turn over decisions to the financial advisor or trust my own instincts?**

Do your research thoroughly, listen to what the advisor has to say, and then trust your instincts. If you feel uneasy about an investment, probe deeper before sinking large amounts of cash into it. If you feel that a brokerage firm is pushing you in a direction that leaves you doubting its intentions, trust that instinct and express your concerns. While it's wise to listen to information from a savvy investment counselor, you are the one who has to live with the consequences, and you have the right to make all of your financial decisions.

Chapter 4

BANKING AND SHORT-TERM INVESTING

MOST BANKS NO longer actively solicit customers by offering deposit gifts, but you can win definite advantages—such as lowered minimum deposit requirements, competitive interest rates, or free checks—that make shopping for a bank worthwhile. The same holds true for short-term investing. This can seem like a lot of comparison-shopping for a small benefit, and yet shopping around raises earning potential that adds up in the long run. Avoiding hidden fees, using higher-yielding bank products, and discovering lucrative short-term investments are simple financial steps that will help you maximize your savings.

Question 34: **What do I need to know about banking?**

Some banks have options that can benefit you, and others charge excessive fees. Rather than selecting a bank for proximity, family tradition, or effective advertising, you can save money by knowing your banking options, how banks function, what practices will incur unnecessary expense, and what practices will help you save money. Your basic choices boil down to the following:

- **Local banks:** These offer the advantage of letting you build a relationship with your banker. They may charge higher fees, but they may also be quicker to handle mistakes or to acquire loans.
- **National banks:** Fees, including ATM charges, may be lower, but these banks may also make more mistakes that require excessive effort on your part to sort out.
- **Savings and loans:** These may offer higher interest rates and loan accessibility, but they may not be as flexible on checking services.
- **Credit unions:** Membership usually requires an affiliation with other credit union members (such as a Chevron credit union for Chevron employees). Credit unions are owned and controlled by the people who use them, as nonprofit organizations. You can find credit unions at *www.creditunion.com*. Because they're nonprofit groups, credit unions can offer rates and loan terms more favorable than those offered through other banks.

Question 35: **What are the typical account options?**

The types of accounts available include the following:

- **Basic checking:** This type of account is used only for bill paying and daily expenses (earns no interest).
- **Interest-bearing checking:** If you can stash and maintain a $1,000 balance, this might be a better option. These accounts pay interest but usually require a minimum balance to offset charges.
- **Basic savings:** Shop for competitive rates and services such as overdraft protection or automatic deposits.
- **Money market:** This type of account combines checking, savings, and investment funds. They usually require a healthy deposit to open, but they may also provide free checks and pay interest.

- **Express:** These accounts can be useful if you use ATM, Internet, or phone for access or to pay bills.
- **Lifeline:** These accounts usually have restricted check writing and are designed for the low-income customer.

Question 36: **What do I need to ask the banking representative?**

As you shop for the best banking opportunities, ask the bank representative the following questions:

- What are the service charges?
- How long does it take for a check to clear?
- What is the overdraft policy?
- What is the interest rate on savings accounts?
- What are the advantages of having a checking or savings account there?

Question 37: **How do automatic bill payments work?**

This is an arrangement you make with your mortgage company, credit cards, insurance companies, and other debtors to withdraw money from your checking account. Money is extracted on a set date each month, until you cancel the arrangement. Make sure you notify credit cards when terminating automatic withdrawals or they will clip you for returned check fees when their bank hits up your bank for the funds. Also make sure you mail credit card payments—at least the minimum amount due—by the due date.

Question 38: **What are scheduled transfers?**

Money is transferred from one account to another, per your instructions. You can opt to have a portion of your direct deposit sent to your savings account, or to have 20 percent of your balance transferred to your savings account on a set date each month.

Question 39: **What are overdrafts?**

When you don't have sufficient money in the account to cover a withdrawal or a check, the bank may pay the amount and charge you a penalty. You need to know the bank's overdraft policy, whether you have overdraft protection, and what it will charge you for overdrafts. You may be able to use your savings as overdraft protection, but—obviously—it's far better to avoid the problem altogether. Overdrafts also mean charges from the bank—and the credit card company or landlord or your doctor—and can affect your credit rating.

Question 40: **What are direct deposits?**

Most employers offer direct deposits for your paychecks. Make sure you know the actual date that the money will land in your account so that you can make sure any automatic deductions or expenses can be fully funded by the due date. Give yourself at least three days leeway to account for glitches.

Question 41: **Once I select an account, what are the most important things I need to do?**

How you watch your money will be as important as how much money you earn. When you receive your bank statements (whether by snail mail or e-mail), it's vitally important that you scour it for errors and validate any charges. If you find errors, you may only have sixty to ninety days to catch and correct them, so it's best to call the bank, and then write a verifying letter so that you have a record for your files. It's imperative that you balance your checking account monthly.

Question 42: **How do I know if my money is safe?**

The Federal Deposit Insurance Corporation (FDIC) insures up to $100,000 per person per FDIC-insured bank (you can check online, at *www.fdic.gov*, to see if your bank is insured). The FDIC also insures up to $250,000 per person, per insured institution for individual retirement accounts (IRAs), as long as the individual owner directs the investment. When a management firm ("plan administrator") controls the investment of employees' IRA assets—as is the case with most company profit-sharing and defined-benefit retirement plan assets—the accounts are not FDIC-insured.

Question 43: **What is short-term liquidity?**

Short-term liquidity means that your cash remains easily accessible. While ideally you are working toward long-term investments, you always want a certain amount of cash available for minor emergencies or blips on the financial radar screen. The smart investor maximizes returns on her cash by choosing money market accounts, or purchasing certificates of deposit or T-bills that earn a higher interest rate than traditional checking or savings accounts.

Question 44: **What is a money market account?**

A money market account is a mutual fund that invests in short-term securities, like U.S. Treasury debt obligations, short-term bonds backed by homeowners' mortgage payments, CDs, and short-term funds lent to large corporations. Many large brokerage firms, banks, and credit unions offer money market accounts that include unlimited check writing and an ATM card.

Question 45: **When do I need a money market account?**

As soon as you accumulate more than $500 in your savings, it's time to deposit the money into an account that will earn competitive interest rates and yet remain liquid (accessible). Many people assume their local banks pay competitive interest rates on savings or checking, and they opt for the comfort of keeping it all under one umbrella. In fact, savings and checking accounts often pay little or no interest, and many have monthly charges that eat away at your savings. Instead, you can house your savings in a money market account that will pay higher, competitive interest and that frequently offers other benefits.

Question 46: **Is there a minimum deposit requirement for money market accounts?**

Money market accounts have been around for eons, but in past decades you had to deposit a minimum of $10,000. Today, they're far more accessible to everyone. Some firms that offer these accounts include Fidelity Investments (minimum investment $2,500), Merrill-Lynch ($2,000), Charles Schwab ($2,500), Morgan Stanley ($2,000), and Edward Jones ($1,000).

Most require a minimum balance of $2,000, but you can find institutions that will open an account with a minimum balance of $500 or even less. Shop around for the best interest rates and perks.

Question 47: **Are there advantages to having my money in a money market account?**

Money market accounts typically offer a higher interest rate than traditional checking or savings accounts, with no hidden charges. Shopping for the highest rate can pay off—some money market accounts pay four times the rate of traditional bank accounts and still offer free checking and ATM cards. Money market funds invested in short-term treasury bonds currently yield about 3.3 percent on average, according to the website *www.bankrate.com*, but yields on any short-term cash investment like a money market or CD will vary over time.

The only downside to money market accounts is that though they are among the safest options, they are not federally insured.

Question 48: **What are certificates of deposit (CDs)?**

Certificates of deposit (CDs) are bank-issued securities that pay a fixed rate of return for a specified period of time, ranging from one month to ten years. The rates may be higher than money market account rates.

They are federally insured up to $100,000; however, they are only as safe as the bank that sells them. To check whether your bank's deposits are safe by virtue of federal government-backed Federal Deposit Insurance Corporation (FDIC) insurance, visit the official website of the FDIC, online at *www.fdic.gov.*

Question 49: **Where do I shop for the best rates on CDs?**

To find the best rates, you rarely need to go further than the Internet. Sites that provide valuable information include *www .bauerfinancial.com*, *www.banked.com*, and *www.bankrate.com*. CDs can also be purchased through brokerage firms, and brokerage firms are more likely to offer liquidity—you may be able to cash in your CDs before the date of maturity by paying a small commission that will be less than the clipping you'll take from traditional banks.

Question 50: **Are there drawbacks to investing in CDs?**

The major disadvantage is that you can rarely withdraw or cash in the CDs before they are due without paying a penalty that cuts severely into your interest earnings. Money market accounts are always liquid, and you are not penalized if you need to withdraw the funds. Therefore, if you find a money market account that pays equal or higher interest rates to comparable CDs, you should choose the money market account.

Question 51: **What are treasury bills (T-bills)?**

Treasury bills (T-bills) are fixed-income securities that can be purchased from the U.S. Treasury Department (*www.publicdebt.treas .gov*) or through a bank or brokerage firm. They are typically issued in $1,000 increments and mature in a year or less. Unlike CDs, T-bills do not pay interest. Instead, they are issued at a discount and are paid in full upon maturity. Thus, you might purchase a $10,000 T-bill for $9,500 and receive $10,000 when you cash it in a year later.

Question 52: **What are the advantages to investing in T-bills?**

Treasury bills are among the safest investments you can buy. T-bills are fully insured by the U. S. government and thus are logically the safest investment. If you buy them through a broker, you can usually sell them via telephone for only a small commission and collect your money within three days.

Question 53: **What is mid-term liquidity?**

Mid-term liquidity means that you can live without tapping into your funds for two to five years. As a result, you can afford to take slightly higher risks. Investing in bonds or treasury notes are a couple of ways to reap higher returns.

Question 54: **What are bonds?**

High-quality government agency bonds are only slightly riskier than money market accounts, CDs, or T-bills. Agency bonds are a loan you make to government agencies (Fannie Mae, Freddie Mac) that write mortgages. The bond serves as an IOU, and it clearly spells out how much you are lending, when the note will mature, and how much interest you will receive. Interest is typically paid in semiannual installments.

Bonds are available in $1,000, $5,000, or $10,000 increments, and they can mature in any time range from one to up to thirty years. Shorter maturities mean lowered risk and lower interest rates. Government bonds are assumed to be the safest in the bond universe.

Question 55: **What are treasury notes?**

Treasury notes are bonds issued by the U.S. government in increments of $1,000. Maturity dates range from two years to ten years. Notes can be bought directly from the government or through brokerage firms. Buying through a brokerage firm will involve paying a commission, but once again, doing so keeps the funds more liquid and outweighs the small price you pay. Treasury note interest payments are exempt from state and local taxes.

Question 56: **What are corporate bonds?**

Rather than the U. S. government, individual corporations sell corporate bonds, and thus the government does not secure, or guarantee, these bonds. Corporate bonds will be as solid as the company that offers them, so it's imperative that you check the company's credit rating. Your broker will be able to tell you what the major credit rating companies say about the rating of the bonds you are considering buying. Ratings from Standard & Poor's, a major bond-rating company, start at AAA (highest credit rating) and descend: AAA-, AA+, AA, AA-, A, and so on. If a company's bond has a rating below BBB-, that bond is considered relatively speculative and not "investment grade." If you are buying individual bonds on your own, stay above a BBB rating.

Question 57: **What are municipal bonds?**

State or local governments issue municipal bonds to pay for public improvements, such as bridges, roads, or schools, or to cover nonspecific short-term government funding shortfalls. Because interest is not subject to federal taxes, or home state taxes when the bond funds a government in your state, investors in high tax brackets benefit most by holding municipal bonds. Gains on municipal bonds, if any, are subject to federal and state taxes. Since they are generally backed by private insurance, municipal bonds are very safe investments. However, highly rated municipal bonds generally offer moderately low rates of interest. They can be useful as a safety valve in balancing higher risk investments and rounding out your portfolio.

Chapter 5

ASSESSING AND CONQUERING YOUR DEBT

NOT ONLY HAS the federal government been overspending, throwing the entire society into a deficit economy, individuals and families have grossly overspent—and grossly overcharged the purchases onto high-interest credit cards. Americans owe $1.7 trillion dollars in personal debt, and one-third of that is credit card debt. If you stacked a pile of $100 bills, a million dollars would reach just over six feet. A billion would be a mile high, and a trillion would skyrocket 350 miles into the stratosphere.

Question 58: Why is it so dangerous to max out my credit cards?

Statistics show that most Americans are staggering under the weight of exceptional credit card debt. Indeed, taken on a national basis, the amount of the debt creates a bleak reality; taken on an individual basis, it's catastrophic. Maxed-out credit cards can easily become a downward spiral that all too quickly becomes a fiscal death spiral for many.

Question 59: **How much debt is acceptable?**

Most financial advisors advocate that consumers have no more than 36 percent of their total gross income allocated to debt repayment—including house payments, car payments, insurance payments, medical payments, credit cards, and student loans. It is important to make smart money decisions by differentiating between good and bad debts—maximizing one and minimizing the other.

Question 60: **Is there such a thing as a good debt?**

Yes, actually, there is. Basically, when a debt vastly increases the actual amount to be paid for a product that doesn't increase in value, it's a bad debt. When debt is used purposefully and intelligently to build wealth, such as to invest in a solid business venture, it's a good debt.

Question 61: **Can a bad debt become a good debt?**

Occasionally. Taking a second mortgage to pay down credit card debt can turn bad debt into good debt, particularly if you get a home equity loan with a tax-deductible, 6-percent interest rate to pay down credit card balances logging 20- to 30-percent interest—provided you pay it off as soon as possible and don't max out your credit cards again. In general, buying a home or refinancing to vastly reduce excessively high interest rates is usually good debt, as is generating limited debt to buy investments that are virtually guaranteed to meet expectations within a short period of time. (Note that stocks can be unexpectedly volatile and rarely justify a home equity loan.) However, always exercise caution and don't run your charge cards up again or you'll defeat the purpose and create bad debt.

Question 62: **Are credit card charges always a bad debt?**

Credit cards generally create bad debt. If you paid off your balances in full every month prior to the end of the grace period, you wouldn't pay any interest and would thus avoid generating bad debt. Unfortunately, few of us are able to pay the balances in full each month. In fact, the vast majority of people overcharge and end up paying the minimum amount due, which immediately generates bad debt. And once you're under the elephant that maxed-out, high-interest credit card debt quickly becomes, it's exceedingly hard to dig your way out—and it's very, very costly.

Question 63: **If they create bad debt, why is it smart to have credit cards?**

Other than convenience, and perhaps minimal protection, the biggest pro to having credit cards is that successful management of three bank cards and two department store accounts can, indeed, bolster your credit rating. However, lenders blanch when they see excessive credit cards, maximization of credit limits, slow payments, late payments, chronic delinquencies, or other worrisome debt repayment habits.

Question 64: **What are the cons to having credit cards?**

The cons frequently far outweigh the pros. Credit card issuers are constantly seeking customers who charge beyond their means and make minimum payments carrying 18- to 30-percent interest for long periods of time. Often the interest charges will double, or even triple, the amount originally charged, making you poor and the credit card company rich.

Question 65: **Why is carrying credit card balances so destructive?**

If you charged $3,000 on your credit card and made minimum payments of $148.50 over the next two years, you would pay an extra $559, adding 18.6 percent to the total cost. With one late fee, your interest and fees could leap to 28 percent, raising your required monthly minimum to $159, and increasing the extra costs to $691, adding 23 percent to the total cost.

Federal interest-rate hikes have increased punitive interest rates (things like late payment fees, over-your-limit fees, returned check fees, or missed payments) 25 to 30 percent in recent years. Also, over-the-limit fees shot up 17 percent from 2001 to 2004 (around $33.50), and grace periods are shrinking (from 28 days to 23 days, or zip on some cards).

Also, when you apply for a loan or seek a new credit card, potential lenders will acquire your credit report and review your debt-to-income ratio. If you have used well beyond 30 percent of the available credit on your credit cards, they may charge you high interest rates, decline your loan, or refuse additional credit.

Question 66: **Even if you rarely use them, can you have too many credit cards?**

Even when you have racked up large balances, credit card companies continue to barrage you with offers, and they all sound tempting, particularly when they offer a low-interest introductory rate. However, be aware that all credit card companies source your credit rating or FICO score to determine your credit worthiness, and all inquiries are registered and may penalize you in the long run.

You have to read the small print—word for word. And you'll have to monitor all of your statements to watch for hidden charges or elevations in your interest rate. Despite ten years of outstanding credit and always paying her bills on time, one month a friend didn't mail the payment in time to reach the company on the due date, and they raised her interest rate to 30 percent—and she didn't even notice for a year!

Question 67: **Are department-store credit cards better or worse than regular credit cards?**

Department stores are always trying to entice you to open an account. What the stores don't tell you is that they may boost your interest rate 15 to 25 percent within months, which means any balances will cost you far, far more than you saved initially. Plus, an excess of department store credit cards on your credit report may diminish your credit worthiness.

Only opt to hold credit cards at stores you shop at often, and limit your choices to two or three at most. If you cannot pay cash or use your debit card, you're better off paying with a bank credit card. Remember: Just say no to department store credit card offers.

Question 68: **Is it a good idea to transfer balances?**

Transferring balances to another card and opening new cards gives you the very false illusion that you can get your debt under control. This is a very bad idea. There is no way to address the problem but to tackle it head on and to cease all credit card spending. In the past, you could declare bankruptcy and wipe the slate relatively clean (never 100 percent) and rebuild your credit score over the course of seven years. However, the government rewrote the bankruptcy laws recently, which means most people have far more limited options to make debt go away.

Question 69: **How do I tackle credit card debt?**

The first thing you have to do is assess your real situation. You cannot tackle the debt until you are ready to make a completely honest appraisal. You need to pull out all your credit card statements; education, car, home, and home equity loan statements;

utility bills; insurance bills; and anything else that documents how much you owe. It's time to record the cold, hard reality of each.

Question 70: **Once I have compiled my credit assessment, what do I do next?**

Compiling the list of accounts also means that it's time for you to get out a magnifying glass and read the fine print. You're looking for the following:

- **Interest rates (APR):** This is the annual percentage you pay for the privilege of using the credit card.
- **Periodic rate:** This is the interest rate you are charged on your purchases or balance each month. You can calculate this by dividing your APR by 12 (months).
- **Finance charge:** This is the monthly fee added to your balance based on the monthly interest rate. Compute it by dividing your APR by 12 and multiplying it by your balance.
- **Grace period:** The amount of time (25 to 28 days) that lapses between when you make the purchase and when you have to pay those charges to avoid interest charges.
- **Fixed versus variable rate:** Most credit cards have variable rates, and the very bad news is that most of them state in the small print on the back of your bill that they can raise your rates at any time, for any reason. You need to monitor this rate so that you can catch hikes in time to minimize damage.
- **Annual fees:** This can include a $40 to $80 fee for the privilege of using the card. Try to find a card that doesn't charge an annual fee—easiest to do when you have good credit.
- **Hidden fees:** If you read the small print, these extra charges are not really hidden. Charges can include balance transfer fees, cash advance fees, special services, and over-your-limit fees, all of which can be excessive.

- **Credit limit:** Remember your target is to get the balance down so that 70 percent of your credit limit is available (but not used!).
- **Consequences:** If you don't pay the bill on time, will you lose your house, your car, or your account? How much will your interest rates increase if you falter—go over your credit limit, slow pay, miss one month, pay less than the minimum, or fail to pay?

Question 71: **Will credit card companies negotiate on terms or a payment schedule?**

Some do! Once you have the credit card accounts ordered, it's time to call each credit card company (or department store) and request a reduction in your interest rate. If you have been a long-term, responsible customer, they may automatically reduce the rate. If the first person you speak with says that they are not authorized to lower the rate, ask to speak to a supervisor. It's wise to maintain a professional, polite tone and calmly ask for what you want. If you still don't get what you want, ask to go another step up the ladder. Persist, and you will often succeed.

Question 72: **How do I decide which credit cards to pay first?**

You need to create an action plan to pay down your debt. Using the assessment table that you created, you need to rate the urgency. For example, things like house payments, car payments, utility bills, and insurance payments take priority over credit card debt. Order your essential (hopefully good) debts so that you will pay the most important bills first. Once again, using the chart you created, allocate funds to pay minimum balances on all the accounts, and then subtract them from your income. Using this figure, deduct your budgeted living expenses to calculate the real amount of income remaining to pay down credit card debt.

Generally, you'll want to pay down the cards with the highest rate of interest first. However, if all of your cards are maxed out, and all the interest rates are in the same range, you may want to distribute funds to bring them all down to a more manageable balance.

Question 73: **Once I pay my credit cards down, should I continue to use them?**

Rarely. Any time you are tempted to whip out a credit card to purchase something that will not increase in value, you can do yourself a big favor: Ask yourself if you could pay cash for it. If you cannot afford to pay for it in cash, then you're better off not buying it.

Chapter **6**

REVIEWING AND REPAIRING YOUR CREDIT REPORT

LIKE IT OR not, your credit history is submitted to three credit reporting agencies, each of which computes a FICO score—a Fair and Isaacs Company formula that has been widely used to assess credit worthiness. This credit rating is used to determine whether you are worthy of the lowest interest rates or whether you are only eligible for secured or high-rate credit. One of your immediate financial goals will be to get, review, and clean up your credit report.

Question 74: **What is a credit report?**

Your credit report is a document that offers potential lenders—or employers, or insurance companies—a report card on your ability to handle debt. It is created as soon as you establish a bank account, begin work, save money, or acquire credit. The information accumulates from day one and can sit there forever. Three credit reporting agencies—Equifax, Experian, and TransUnion—gather and dispense your credit information. (Addresses for all three are available in Appendix B.) You are entitled to one free report a year.

Go online to *www.annualcreditreport.com* to request one free report from each of the three agencies.

Although there are smaller companies that collect credit data, one—or all three—of the major credit reporting agencies will have 90 percent of your credit information on file.

Question 75: **What information is in my credit report?**

Your credit report contains the following:

- Personal information
- Credit information
- Public information
- Inquiry information

This is all information you will want to review carefully when you receive a copy of your credit report.

Question 76: **Do I have any rights when it comes to my credit report?**

The Fair Credit Reporting Act (FCRA) was put in place to protect your privacy and establish rules for the collecting, reporting, and altering of information in your credit file. If you've been turned down for a loan, you can get a copy of the report that generated negative information that had an impact on the lender's decision free of charge. The law requires the credit reporting agencies to respond to your inquiries within thirty days of receipt of your complaint. They are required to investigate the matter free of charge and record the status of the disputed item or to delete the item from your credit report. Typically, they will mail a letter to the creditor to verify that the information is correct. If the creditor cannot validate the charges, the credit reporting agencies are required to delete the item from your report and notify other agencies. They are also required to remove any information that pertains to someone else, correct any inaccurate information, and remove duplicate information.

Question 77: **What do I do if I find an error?**

A relatively reasonable 30 to a whopping 90 percent of credit reports are said to have some inaccuracies. If you find substantial errors on one report, it's important to get, check, and clear all three reports individually. To clean up your credit reports, do the following:

- Write a letter to each of the three credit reporting agencies listing the errors. The addresses are in Appendix B.
- Attach copies of supporting documentation (cancelled checks, statements).
- Send the letter via certified mail, return receipt requested.
- Keep a copy for your files, and attach the receipt confirmation when it arrives.
- Follow up with telephone calls, if needed.

Question 78: **What if the credit agencies don't correct the errors?**

Keep in mind that you're dealing with a bureaucracy that isn't in the business of correcting reports. You will need to follow up religiously and hound them until the corrections have been made. Once the corrections have been made, the credit reporting agencies are required to send you a copy of your corrected report free of charge. If you request it, they are also required to send the updated report to anyone who received it in the last six months, or, if the requester was an employer, the last two years.

Question 79: **Should I hire someone else to clean up my credit report?**

Be wary of companies offering to clean up your credit report. No one has a magic wand they can wave over your credit history. They would have to go through the same steps you would—and easily can—do for free.

Also, be wary of companies that offer free FICO scores. These offers usually lead to long-term credit monitoring that isn't free. Also, never send your personal information to an unknown company over the Internet. If you need to order your report more than once a year, be safe and pay the $12.95 per report on *www.myfico. com.*

Question 80: **Once an item is removed, is it gone forever?**

Once a disputed item has been removed, the credit agencies are not permitted to put it back on your report without sending you written notification and alerting you to the name, address, and telephone number of the creditor submitting the item. You are always free to write directly to the creditor to dispute the information. You can place a copy of this letter in your credit file. The creditor is also required to include a notice of dispute if it submits the information again after you have disputed it. If the disputed item was not verified, the creditor is not permitted to submit the item again.

Question 81: **What if problematic items are my debts?**

As far as legitimate items that reflect badly on your credit worthiness, you can make efforts to improve them. Bankruptcies will sit on your report for ten years; missteps like late payments will stay for seven years. Criminal convictions may remain in place for decades, as will applications for jobs that pay more than $75,000 (which may require a background and credit check by the employer) or applications for credit or life insurance for more than $150,000.

Even if you were guilty of late payments, overdrafts, or long-running delinquencies, you can still write to the credit agencies requesting that they verify the negative posting. In some cases, the entries may be so old that the creditor may not verify them, which means they will remove the items from your credit report.

Question 82: **Can I still appeal to have items removed?**

Creditors are not required by law to report everything pertaining to your account. You can certainly write to the department store, utility company, or credit card company to plead your case. Perhaps you were unemployed for three months back in 2002 and ran late on your accounts. If you write to the creditors noting that you have been an excellent customer—who has paid $1,200 in interest payments, and who rectified that situation and has kept the account current for the past three years—they may opt to remove the negative report.

Question 83: **What if they deny my request?**

If your initial inquiry elicits a negative response, write to the president of the company expressing dismay that they have refused to help and again noting how much interest you have paid and the overall health of your account and your paying habits. All you are asking for is for them to write a letter to the credit reporting agencies, and it's not an unreasonable request.

Question 84: **Should I settle old accounts?**

If you have a long-standing unpaid bill, and you are applying for home financing, you may want to offer a settlement in return for a clean slate. Creditors often leap at offers to pay half of the original amount, particularly if it's been hanging out there a long time. If you do this, however, it is vitally important that you request a letter from the creditor agreeing to the terms of the settlement in return for wiping the slate clean. Don't pay them until you have a written record that they are accepting this payment as final payment on money due. You want them to report that you are "paying the account in full." If they fail to clear your credit report, you will need this letter to clear it.

Question 85: **When should I hire a lawyer?**

If you have a lot of old debts, it may be wise to hire a lawyer to negotiate repayment. In some cases, the old debts may disappear seven years after the last payment, and inquiries may reopen them. Lawyers will know how to negotiate settlements without stirring up the dust, which could save you hundreds, or thousands, of dollars and prevent negative items from reappearing.

Question 86: **What if all my efforts fail?**

If singing your sad (but true) song fails to motivate the creditors to assist you, the Fair Credit Reporting Act allows consumers to write a short explanation disputing or explaining the history to the credit reporting agencies, who are required to place it in your file. Keep it simple and no longer than 100 words. Sample notations might read as follows: "Late payment was due to move and subsequent lost mail"; "Laid off from work for six months, caught up all accounts upon returning to work"; "Emergency occurred while out of the country, tripled payments upon return."

Question 87: **What if I have positive items that I would want to have on my credit report?**

You can also write positive notes that the agencies are required to send to all inquiries. Samples would include things like these: "I received a $10,000 raise in 2005," or "I earned an extra $7,000 in sales commissions in the first quarter of 2006."

Chapter 7

IMPROVING YOUR FICO SCORE

AS WE MENTIONED in the previous chapter there are three credit reporting agencies—Experian, TransUnion, and Equifax—each of which computes a FICO score—a Fair and Isaacs Company formula that has been widely used to assess credit worthiness. This credit rating is vitally important to your financial health. It will determine whether you are worthy of the lowest interest rates or whether you are only eligible for secured or high-rate credit. This could mean the difference between having an affordable mortgage, and having to pay thousands of dollars more due to a low FICO score. One of your ultimate financial goals will be to boost and safeguard your FICO scores.

Question 88: **What is a FICO score?**

The three crediting reporting agencies mentioned earlier collect and compile information about your credit history and submit it to formulas—which can vary wildly—that will create your FICO score.

In fact, mortgage lenders have used FICO scores for years as a predictor of consumers' future bill-paying performance, which determines whether they grant loans and at what interest rate. Today, insurance companies, cell-phone providers, utilities, landlords, and even prospective employers may use your FICO score as an indicator of your stability, trustworthiness, and ability to pay your bills on time.

Question 89: **What determines my FICO score?**

FICO collects twenty-two pieces of data from each of the three credit bureaus to tabulate an individual's score. The final number is a composite of individual ratings in five categories:

1. Payment history (35 percent)
2. Amount of outstanding debt (30 percent)
3. Length of credit history (15 percent)
4. Amount of newly acquired credit (10 percent)
5. Types of credit used (10 percent)

Question 90: **Does my income have any effect on my FICO score?**

Surprisingly, your annual income doesn't even figure into the equation. Someone could have a very high income and rarely pay her bills on time; conversely, someone could earn an average income but possess a long, stellar payment record. What they are looking for is a long, stable, responsible, well-managed history with credit.

Question 91: **Do each of the three agencies have the same score?**

No. Each of the three major agencies computes an individual FICO score for you, and because they don't share information, it's crucial that you get and monitor all three scores. Seventy-five percent of mortgage companies will request all three scores when determining your credit worthiness, and each may have its own scoring formula that it uses to determine your credit worthiness.

Question 92: **What is a good FICO score?**

FICO scores typically range from a high of 850 to a low of 300. Seventy percent of consumers have scores above 600. Average scores hover around 720. Borrowers with scores above 740 generally receive the best rates.

Question 93: **Why is it important to have a high FICO score?**

The higher your FICO score, the lower risk you appear to a creditor, which translates into lower interest rates for your loan. For example, if you score in the 740 to 850 range, lenders might offer you a $350,000, thirty-year fixed mortgage at 6.24 percent interest, which would result in a mortgage of $2,153 a month. However, if you score between 620 and 674, the lender would charge closer to 8.05 percent, raising your monthly mortgage to $2,581. You would pay an additional $150,000 over the life of the loan.

Question 94: **How do I find out my FICO score?**

Each of the three reporting agencies is required to give you one free credit report annually, and all three will offer to calculate a credit score for a slight fee. Even though their individual scores will not truly represent your FICO score, they will give you a real idea of how lenders will assess your score. To get the most realistic picture of your FICO standing, click on "credit education" at *www.myfico .com*, and order all three scores.

Question 95: **Why should I order my FICO score?**

When you order a report from the credit reporting agencies or *www.myfico.com*, the report provides a list of positive and negative elements that have affected your score. If your score is particularly low, these lists will provide valuable information for improving it.

Question 96: **How often should I request my FICO score?**

It's a great idea to check your FICO scores once a year; and if you're in the market for a mortgage, order them at least four months ahead so you can clean up any problems.

Even though negative history—late payments, delinquencies, liens, and judgments against you—will adversely affect your FICO score for up to seven years, most lenders scrutinize the past two years, minimizing the effect of one thirty-day late payment.

Obviously, you want to maximize positive history. If your FICO score is on the low end, you'll want to create a plan to address the problems and reverse the trend. However, it behooves every consumer to do everything possible to boost her FICO score.

Question 97: **How are my FICO scores used?**

FICO scores are used for many purposes, such as:

- Predicting your credit paying habits
- Predicting the likelihood that you will default on loans
- Predicting which accounts you would be likely to pay first (utility, insurance, home, auto, credit cards)
- Predicting whether you will file insurance claims
- Detecting fraud in insurance or credit applications
- Calculating how much profit a credit company will earn from you
- Noting whether you are likely to respond to credit offers via mail

Question 98: **What damages my FICO score?**

Although FICO scores and how creditors evaluate or use them in their full assessment can vary widely, there are definite actions that will negatively affect your FICO score. The following may create red flags or drop your FICO score:

- Moving around a lot (residences and jobs)
- Slow payment or missing payments
- Minimum credit history
- Too many outstanding balances
- Too much available credit
- Too many inquiries

Question 99: **How do I improve my FICO score?**

Rest assured, you can definitely improve upon and bolster a flagging FICO score. Revitalizing your FICO score is as easy as taking these steps:

- Paying all of your bills on time
- Keeping your balances low
- Establishing a positive history
- Minimizing credit card or loan applications
- Not consolidating to take advantage of lower interest rates
- Not charging new debt
- Thinking twice before closing accounts
- Paying off small balances

Question 100: **When and how do I take drastic measures?**

If you cannot meet your monthly expenses, it's time to severely tighten your belt. First, you'll need to review your budget in light of your expenditures. If your income is falling short, you'll need to adjust spending radically and immediately. If you absolutely cannot squeeze your expenses sufficiently to cover all of your debts, you may want to work with a credit management company that would tailor a payment program to your needs.

Question 101: **What if I need help resolving my debt?**

If you need help resolving debt, credit management agencies will work directly with your creditors to establish a payment plan. Many will consolidate your payments, collect the money from you, and pay your bills. It's crucial that you do some preliminary research to make sure you find a reputable agency. Contact the National Foundation for Consumer Credit, online at *www.nfcc.org*, for more information specific to credit management.

Question 102: **If I work with a credit management company, will it affect my FICO score?**

It might. Beware of signing on too quickly for debt management programs initiated by credit agencies. Most will report the debt management program to the credit reporting agencies, meaning it will show up on your credit history. If you have substantial debt, the benefit may outweigh the risk, but ask your counselor if reporting can be avoided.

Question 103: **What do I look for in a credit management agency?**

Look for one that tailors a solution to your problems, rather than one that takes the easiest or most profitable solution—one that would benefit the agency and the creditors. If they have more than 50 percent of their clients on debt management programs, they're not trying hard enough to find individualized solutions. You also want one that has debt management training programs that will help you establish healthy financial habits. Also, shop around for an accredited agency with trained and certified counselors. If you feel strong-armed, or unheard, trust your instincts. Your credit history is an asset you need to protect.

Question 104: **If I'm in a pinch, should I take out a loan to pay my credit cards?**

No. You've all seen the commercials on television suggesting that it's easy for anyone who suffers a calamity to call a phone number to acquire a quick $10,000 to cover her escalating bills. Anyone in this situation is already in over her credit head, i.e., a high-risk borrower who has had trouble paying her debts and will most likely continue to default on future payments. The lenders who offer loans to high-risk borrowers charge them exorbitant interest rates and steep penalties for late payment.

Question 105: **When should I look for another job?**

If you've cut expenses down to the bone and still cannot meet your debts, it's time to look for a second job. Use your creativity to come up with a list of part-time jobs you could seek (or create) to supplement your income—bartending, babysitting, dog walking, freelance typing, interior decorating, personal shopping, cleaning, gardening, garage sale organization, or plain old errand running. Do whatever it takes to pay down your debt and maintain a solid credit rating. Everyone falls on hard times, but it's up to you how you navigate the territory. Keep in mind the long-term effects, and choose the high road.

Chapter 8

AVOIDING IDENTITY THEFT

IDENTITY THEFT HAS become an American scourge—it's the number-one consumer complaint. Although always a problem, it has surged in recent years, largely because of electronic commerce. All a thief needs is your Social Security number, your address, your birth date, and a little family information to open credit cards in your name. Unfortunately, avoiding identity theft is not as easy as safeguarding your Social Security number—although it's essential to do so. Today, you need consciousness and diligence to protect your credit identity, credit history, and FICO score.

Question 106: **What is identity theft?**

Identity theft occurs when someone takes your private information—Social Security number, driver's license number, credit card numbers, bank account numbers, place of employment, and even family information, such as your mother's maiden name—and uses that information to pillage your bank and credit card accounts or to open new accounts using your information.

Question 107: **How often does identity theft really occur?**

According to Liz Pulliam Weston, author of *Your Credit Score*, identity theft affects more than 10 million people a year. The Federal Trade Commission survey found that 27.3 million Americans had become victims of identity theft in the past five years. This results in $48 billion in annual losses for business and institutions; $5 billion in out-of-pocket expenses for consumers; and 300 million hours spent by consumers trying to cope with its consequences. It's wise to take precautions and stay vigilant about protecting your personal and financial identity.

Question 108: **How does identity theft occur?**

The most common ways that information is stolen are as follows:

- Someone you typically trust (a waiter at a restaurant, or a salesperson in a retail store) scans your credit card into a handheld device called a "skimmer" and uses or sells the information to open bogus accounts.
- Someone confiscates, or finds, your applications for credit, an apartment, insurance, or employment and sells it to identity thieves. Dumpster divers know where to look for such applications.
- Hackers break into databases where your information is stored.
- Bogus companies pose as lenders and call or e-mail you (and often the credit reporting agencies), requesting your credit information.

Question 109: **How do I protect myself from identity theft?**

Although there's no way to completely eliminate the risk, you definitely want to take steps to protect your identity.

- First and foremost, purchase an inexpensive shredder
- Don't print personal information on checks
- Put a lock on your mailbox
- Never leave behind or throw away credit card receipts
- Keep all of your important records under lock and key
- Just say "no" to unsolicited telephone, e-mail, or snail mail credit offers

Question 110: **What's the most important information that I should safeguard?**

The most important information to safeguard includes your mother's maiden name, your Social Security number, PINs, credit card numbers, and preapproved credit card offers. Also, never choose an obvious password, such as your name or your birth date. Instead, choose something obscure—your dog's name, your favorite flower, or your preferred coffee blend, for example.

Question 111: **How do I protect my Social Security number?**

Be extremely selective about giving anyone your Social Security number. The only entities entitled to it are your employer, financial institutions (your bank or brokerage firm when you open an account, for instance), the Department of Motor Vehicles, some governmental agencies, and a small number of other institutions.

Question 112: **How can I protect my credit cards?**

Use one credit card for all online purchases and arrange it so that you can view the account online at any time. Check the balance and all charges once a week to make sure you are the only one using the account. Call credit card companies the moment you notice a card missing.

Question 113: **Is it safe to use my ATM card?**

Guard your ATM card! Thieves can use them to wipe out your checking or savings accounts in seconds. Generally, it's better to use your credit cards more often than your ATM or debit cards, and minimize use of either for small purchases, particularly in fast food restaurants, gas stations, or other businesses where employees may succumb to the temptation to steal information.

Question 114: **Is it safe to provide information over the telephone or Internet?**

No and no! This is vitally important—never provide your financial information to unknown callers. Never presume it's really your bank or credit card company calling. If they say they are reporting a problem, hang up, pull out your statement, and call them directly. And be discreet when supplying your financial information to known sources via cell phone. You never know who's listening.

As far as the Internet, if you initiate the request and know the institution is legitimate, you're probably safe, but keep in mind that technology allows wily criminals to create "look-alike" websites that are virtually identical to your real bank or credit card provider's site.

Question 115: **How can I detect identity theft?**

Monitor your credit reports carefully. Stagger the free reports you are entitled to from each of the three credit reporting agencies, and review them for any errors. Credit monitoring businesses are an option, but they are usually costly; you can monitor your own credit for a fraction of the cost. Be sure to check the section of your report titled "inquiries" to see if a flurry of inquiries regarding opening new credit card accounts has been occurring.

Question 116: **How can I prevent anyone from hacking into my computer?**

To safeguard your computer, regularly upgrade virus software and install a firewall program to protect personal information stored on your computer. Only download files or click on hyperlinks sent by people you know. Stick to secure browsers that use an encryption code—look for the "lock" icon on the browser's status bar. Also, if you store information on your laptop, use a "log-in" feature that requires a user name and password. When you dispose of your computers, delete all files with a "wipe" utility program that overwrites the hard drive.

Question 117: **What if my identity has been stolen?**

If you discover that your identity has been stolen, you must take immediate action. Get ready to make a series of telephone calls and keep meticulous records of every conversation you have. You will relay this same information when you follow up with letters—which you will send certified mail, return receipt requested. Also, keep track of the hours you spend in case the thief is caught and forced to pay retribution (including paying for your time). Begin by contacting the Federal Trade Commission (FTC) at *www .consumer.gov/idtheft.com* to get free information on what you need to do.

Question 118: **When should I call a lawyer?**

Once you have taken all the measures possible, if any problems persist, hire a lawyer, and don't surrender any ground. You are a victim of a crime, not the offender, and you deserve the respect and support of the creditors. Collection agencies have strict guidelines on how they are permitted to seek payment. If a collector becomes threatening or abusive, let her know that she is breaking the law.

Chapter **9**

BUDGETING FOR WEALTH

ALTHOUGH MANY PEOPLE will actually earn a million dollars in their lifetimes, few will be able to transmute it into a fortune. Cornered by debt, many Americans are now forced to work harder just to keep afloat. Largely because of mass overconsumption and irresponsible financial management, we have turned what was once a blissful, hopeful, conceivable American dream into a nation of citizens who are "just getting by." Clearly, if you want to develop wealth, you have to buck the trend and map out your own path to financial health, wealth, and happiness.

Question 119: **If I want to budget for wealth, how do I begin?**

First and foremost, you have to live within your means. According to Stacy Johnson, author of *Life or Debt*, becoming wealthy has nothing whatsoever to do with income or investment knowledge. Accumulating wealth comes from avoiding debt, living below your means, and investing sensibly and consistently. Indeed, says Johnson, "becoming financially independent isn't really a function of how much money you make; it's far more often a function of how little money you spend."

Question 120: **How do I become a smart consumer?**

Those hoping to accumulate wealth understand that carefully considering all expenditures is one of the fastest ways to save money. Ask yourself some basic questions before you buy virtually anything:

- Is this item or service I'm buying really necessary?
- Can I purchase this item or service at a discount?
- Is this expenditure adding to my wealth or detracting from it?

Question 121: **Once my spending is under control, what's the next step?**

Once you know your real situation and adjust your spending, you need to establish financial goals. These goals differ from the goals you set to get your finances in order. These goals are about finding ways to accumulate wealth. Note, however, that you don't want your goals to be too general, as in simply increasing your income by 10 percent; you want to be specific, as in creating a new income stream based on your ability to create handmade jewelry that you can sell monthly at a local flea market. In other words, you want to set concrete goals that can be achieved.

Question 122: **Once I have goals, what do I do first?**

Goals without a written game plan to achieve them are just words on paper. Just as it's important to break down dreams into concrete goals, it's also important to break down all the likely steps you will need to take and obstacles you will need to overcome. Here are the tasks involved:

- Identify necessary steps that will lead up to achieving the goals
- Identify all conceivable obstacles you will have to overcome

- Write down your game plan for mastering the steps
- Write down your game plan for overcoming the obstacles

Question 123: **What constitutes realistic savings goals?**

Even with small amounts added to your investment accounts each month, your savings can grow to be prodigious sums over a few years' time. For instance, at an interest rate of 8 percent, $150 saved per month will become $50,641 in fifteen years. Keep in mind, if you are putting away 10 percent of your monthly salary, and can add another 10 percent from additional income streams, you would essentially double your savings, and increase your chances of becoming a millionaire seven years ahead of schedule.

Question 124: **How do I monitor my progress?**

Goals need a timeframe. It's important to stay on top of your fluctuating reality and to assess how you're doing in terms of meeting your goals. Rather than lapse into unconscious—or unexamined— behavior patterns, keep yourself fully conscious and motivated by reviewing your situation at least quarterly. If you are falling short, make any necessary adjustments.

Question 125: **How do I grow my savings over time?**

Chances are that if you're reading this book, you have decades before you retire to grow your assets, which is certainly enough time to create a substantial nest egg. In the world of investing, there's nothing more important than long stretches of time to make your assets grow. For instance, if you put $1,000 into savings today and earn 6 percent per year (after taxes and fees), in ten years you'll have made a 79-percent return; in twenty years you'll have made a 221-percent return; and in forty years your gain will be 928 percent—and your initial investment will have grown to $10,280! If you earn 8 percent every year for forty years, your $1,000 initial investment will grow to be $21,720—which shows you how much difference 3 percent can make. These kinds of potential returns make starting investing as soon as possible the only feasible way for most of us to retire, or even be considered rich.

Question 126: **How can I make my money grow faster while leveraging my risk?**

Your money will grow faster, and you will take on less risk, if you maintain a diversified portfolio. Diversification should be done both across asset classes—investing in stocks and bonds, and also within asset classes—putting money to work in large and small stocks, and low and high-quality bonds.

Question 127: **If I'm between the ages of twenty and thirty, how should I invest?**

Lucky you! Time is on your side on all fronts. By establishing healthy savings and investing habits, you can build a very bright future for yourself and your children. Even putting $100 a month into a savings account will build into a sizeable amount. If you set aside $250 a month and you earn no interest on the money, you will accumulate $30,000 in ten years! If you put that same amount into savvy investments, such as money market accounts, certificates of deposit, bonds, stocks, or mutual funds, you should earn higher rates of return, maximizing savings.

If you are twenty-two years old and deposit $4,000 a year ($333.33 a month) into a retirement account growing at an 8-percent annual return, those funds would build to $1 million by age sixty-two. If you wait until you're thirty-two, you'd have to more than double the amount to $8,800 a year ($733.33 a month) to reach $1 million by sixty-two.

Question 128: **How do I invest if I'm between the ages of thirty and forty?**

Whether you are twenty-five or thirty-five years away from retirement, time is on your side. Even starting from scratch, there's still time to be a millionaire; however, by waiting longer to get started, you'll need to save $500 per month starting at age thirty, or $1,150 per month at age forty and get an 8-percent return to become a millionaire by age sixty-five.

The good news is that you have decades before you retire, so you can place your savings in higher risk investments that will earn more than 8 percent a year. You'll also have time to recover from a setback if the stock or bond markets stumble.

Question 129: **How do I invest if I'm between the ages of forty and fifty?**

You're older, wiser, and still have fifteen to thirty years until retirement, key years to grow your assets so that when you reach fifty, sixty, and beyond, you'll have enough socked away to fund your expenses and whatever unknowns you encounter. Invest 60 to 70 percent of your funds in stock. You still have time to come back from setbacks, and should have some exposure to riskier stock classes, perhaps 20 to 30 percent of your stock holdings. Invest the remaining 30 to 40 percent in bonds. If you're fifty with no savings and want to be a millionaire in fifteen years, you have to save $2,970 per month and invest it so it grows at 8 percent every year.

Question 130: **How do I invest if I'm between the ages of fifty and sixty?**

You're aged to perfection, and retirement is just around the corner. If you haven't yet done so, it's imperative that you build a nest egg. Because you will soon begin to sell off parts of your portfolio to fund retirement needs and desires, it's time for you to dial down the risk level of your portfolio. You might consider having 55 to

65 percent of your portfolio in stocks if you are fifteen years from retirement, and a lower percentage each year as you approach the big date. It's still important in most cases to own stock and other risky assets in retirement if you have enough money and emotional security to tolerate the volatility.

Question 131: **How do I invest if I'm less than ten years from retirement?**

If you are less than ten years from retiring, consult with a financial advisor to evaluate your asset allocation plan in detail, focusing on what and how much you will need to have in place before you are able to retire. If you haven't saved enough, you may have to drastically cut back on expenses in order to maintain your lifestyle in retirement. You may have to downsize, trading your present house for a less expensive one or even moving to an area where living expenses are substantially less.

Question 132: **If I inherit a significant amount of cash, how do I handle the sudden influx of money?**

If you are lucky enough to inherit property, you are essentially being given a cash cow. Here's what you need to know to maximize the windfall:

- **Estate taxes:** According to current tax laws, unless your total inheritance surpasses $2 million, you will not owe estate taxes. The applicable tax law varies by year—for instance, the nontaxable amount of an estate received in 2007 is $2 million, but in 2010 the estate tax will be repealed—so check with the IRS or a tax professional if you are uncertain, or if your gains exceed $2 million.
- **Market value:** When you inherit property, the property's cost basis is adjusted upward to the current market value. You will need a professional appraiser to determine the

house's market value when it's inherited. It may make sense to sell inherited property quickly—your gain on the sale will be whatever price you receive, less the stepped-up cost basis of the home, so a quick sale could reduce your taxable gains and the cost of upkeep. The $250,000 tax shelter on real estate gains doesn't apply in this case unless you've lived in the house for two of the five years before it is sold.

Question 133: **What are the seven rules for creating wealth?**

If you want to acquire wealth, first and foremost, you have to decide to be wealthy. Choice signals a journey, but it's a commitment to the path that makes all the difference. Follow the seven basic rules, below, and you'll be well on your way.

1. Accept responsibility for your financial future
2. Pay yourself first
3. Know what your money is doing
4. Reduce spending
5. Earn more at your job
6. Generate additional income streams
7. Invest wisely

It's not easy to make the sacrifices, but once you become more enthused about how much money you're saving, savvy about the investments you make, and cognizant of where you are on the financial path versus where you want to be, you'll have a far better chance of becoming wealthy and living to enjoy the benefits.

Chapter **10**

DECIDING WHETHER TO RENT OR OWN

HOMES AND CARS are the most expensive items you will likely purchase. Owning a home is part of the American dream and can be the fastest road to financial security, but it also comes with some big caveats. The decisions you make—whether you lease, rent, or own and when, where, and how you buy—will have a huge impact on your finances. If you make smart money-savvy decisions, one day you will be able to afford your dream car or home.

Question 134: **Are there times when it makes sense to rent rather than buy?**

Renting makes sense when you plan on staying in the home less than five years. Homes rarely accumulate enough equity in the first five years of ownership to make them the highly profitable investment they become if you live in them for longer than that. If your life is unsettled and likely to remain so, the flexibility of being able to leave with one month's advance notice has distinct advantages—such as being able to buy the right property at the right time, or to transfer to another city for a job opening.

Question 135: **What are the drawbacks to renting?**

Renting doesn't make sense for everyone. Without rent control, you may face large and arbitrary annual rent increases. In rare circumstances, a landlord may evict tenants for subjective reasons—such as wanting to move into your home. Finally, as a renter, you don't accrue equity in your home, which for most homeowners translates into the largest asset they own and a major cushion when it comes time to retire.

Question 136: **What are the positive reasons for home ownership?**

The reasons for home ownership are substantial. They include:

- Equity accrual
- Tax breaks
- Fixed costs
- Return-on-investment potential

Question 137: **What are some of the drawbacks to home ownership?**

While a home can be your largest asset, home ownership brings substantial responsibility. In addition to paying a monthly mortgage, you will face insurance, state and local property taxes, landscaping maintenance, routine house and appliance maintenance, and large, unexpected repairs or restorations. Once you own a house, it's crucial that you protect the investment, which can be costly.

Question 138: **Why does it take so long to build equity in my home?**

Part of every mortgage payment goes to interest, which you don't benefit from, and part goes to principal, which pays down your debt.

Over the first ten years of a fixed thirty-year mortgage, you'll pay between 9 and 18 percent to principal, while during the mortgage's final ten years 63 to 72 percent of your payments go to principal. Thus, unless the markets rise in value, it's likely that you won't pay enough principal to build equity until you have owned the house for at least five years.

Question 139: **Is it smarter to buy a condo instead of a house?**

A condominium, particularly in an urban setting, may be a good place to start. Typically, condos cost 20 to 30 percent less than individual homes, and you may be able to minimize your commute and your maintenance costs—both in terms of dollars and hours. The downside includes adherence to the condominium complex's rules, which may restrict exterior paint or landscaping and may even extend to the number of pets you own. Sound from your neighbor's units may also be a turn-off. Keep in mind that condominiums usually have additional monthly fees earmarked for building repairs and other communal expenses.

Question 140: **What should I avoid when buying a condo?**

Beware of buying condos in cities where multiple large condominium complexes are being built. Many of them are purchased by investors who will be quick to dump them during a market downturn, and their interiors and views are pretty standard, which means buyers may not care whether they get the condo on the third or fifth floor. When flooded with undifferentiated condominiums, market prices decline.

Question 141: **What do I need to consider when buying a home?**

Buying a home is both a solid investment strategy and a way to gain stability and enjoyment, but it involves a lot of money and a time commitment. As such, it's wise to make the decision based on meaningful criteria. Begin with a list of what you most want from the home and community in which you will live, as follows:

- Size
- Style
- Essentials
- Schools
- Transportation
- Safety
- Amenities
- Neighbors

In terms of investment potential, location of the property may be the most important determination.

Question 142: **What's the difference between prequalification and preapproval?**

Many people consult with a mortgage lender, who gives them an estimate on what she believes the buyer can afford. This is helpful to you, but if you are ready to buy, going from prequalification to preapproval is advisable. Here's the basic difference:

- Prequalification is an estimate of how much you can borrow that a lender calculates based upon simple data you supply about your income, debt, and debt payments.
- Preapproval is a lender's promise to provide a loan up to a certain amount. Lenders collect and then verify information about your income, debt, and debt payment claims to

determine the amount they are willing to loan you for a home purchase.

Question 143: **How do lenders determine my eligibility to buy a home?**

Lenders evaluate your monthly income, the stability of your monthly income, your monthly debt payments, your assets, and your credit history to determine the maximum amount they are willing to lend you for a particular home. Also, lenders have their own method for computing how much they will loan to you. If you have worked for your current employer for a few years and have a solid credit history, they will probably go as high as 29 percent of your pretax income for mortgage, insurance, and property taxes. However, it's important for you to do your own calculations and decide what you feel you can afford.

Question 144: **Should I shop around to find the lowest interest rate?**

Definitely! Never rely solely on the recommendation of your Realtor or loan agent. Small savings on a large mortgage can add up quickly. Seek out a "lowest-cost bid" for your mortgage through multiple lenders, including your bank and local credit unions that may offer lower-than-average rates. Ask your real estate broker for suggestions, but keep in mind that he or she may favor lenders for reasons other than reliable low-cost loans.

At least three months before you seek preapproval for a mortgage loan, check your credit reports to see if there are any blemishes or mistakes. Using the information in Chapters 5, 6, and 7, make any corrections and clear up anything that will lower your credit score.

Question 145: **How do I determine what I can afford?**

Online mortgage affordability calculators, such as the one at *www.rebuz.com*, will give you an idea of the size of a loan you can afford to finance a home purchase. A calculator from a reputable source should include charges for your current payments on other debts, state and local taxes, and home insurance as part of the calculation.

Question 146: **What is the minimum requirement for a down payment?**

You may be required to invest 10 to 20 percent of the home's value as a down payment for standard home loans to avoid paying private mortgage insurance. That's despite, or perhaps as a result of, the sub-prime debacle. However, if you borrow using mortgages backed by the Federal Housing Administration (FHA) or Veterans' Affairs (VA), you may be able to pay 5 percent, or less, of the home's value in a down payment. The FHA or VA may also help lower your mortgage costs.

Question 147: **How does one qualify for FHA-insured or VA-insured loans?**

If you haven't owned a home within the last three years, if you are divorced and only owned property while married, or if you have only owned a mobile home, you may qualify for an FHA-insured loan. Maximum loans range from $200,000 to $363,000 based on the location of your home. You can calculate your maximum by going online to the U.S. Housing and Urban Development website, at *www.hud.gov*.

VA-insured loans are generally offered only to current and past U.S. military personnel who are currently serving, or who served and were not dishonorably discharged from twenty-four months of active duty, including ninety days of service in wartime or 181 days in peacetime. National Guard and Selected Reserves members with at least six years of service are also eligible for VA loans, as are unmarried spouses of veterans who died while in service. The VA will insure loans up to $203,000 and may not require any down payment.

Question 148: **What is private mortgage insurance?**

Generally, if you invest less than 20 percent of the home's value in a down payment, you will be required to buy private mortgage insurance (PMI). This can cost as much as $500 per year for every $100,000 of mortgage value to insure the lender against your defaulting on the loan. PMI is automatically cancelled when the amount of your outstanding mortgage falls below 78 percent of the home's purchase value; however, you can contact the mortgage lender when your balance is below 80 percent of the home's purchase value to terminate PMI early.

You may be able to get around PMI requirements by taking out an 80-10-10 loan, in which you pay 10 percent of the home's value, take out a higher-interest loan for 10 percent, and then seek a traditional mortgage without PMI for the remaining 80 percent. This may save you money by eliminating years of PMI payments.

Question 149: **What are my mortgage options?**

Lenders typically offer home mortgages that are either fifteen or thirty years with fixed or adjustable interest rates. But the length is negotiable and should be chosen based upon your ability to meet the monthly payments—the shorter the better. The two basic options are as follows:

- Fixed mortgages lock in an interest rate for the life of the loan, which means your monthly payment will not fluctuate.
- Adjustable-rate mortgages (ARMs) offer low fixed initial rates that are adjusted upward after a few years.

Question 150: **What are points?**

You may be offered mortgages with different interest rates based on the number of up-front fees, or "points," you pay to the lender. Paying one point means that you pay the lender 1 percent of the total loan amount when the loan is made. The more points, the lower your interest rate. If you are certain that you will stay in the house for seven to ten years, paying more in up-front points will probably be your best option. The details will vary based on the rate break per point, which will vary by lender. You can find out how long you would have to stay in the house to benefit from paying extra points through an online calculator such as the one at *www.rebuz.com.*

Question 151: **What is amortization?**

It is important to understand the amortization schedule for your mortgage. For a thirty-year fixed mortgage with a 7-percent interest rate, 81 percent of the first twelve years of mortgage payments go toward interest, enriching the mortgage lender. Over the next twelve years, 56 percent of your payments go to interest. In the final six years of the mortgage, only 9 percent of your payments are for interest, while the remaining 91 percent is applied to paying down the balance of your mortgage. The same shift between interest and principal credit over time applies to most mortgages (not interest-only mortgages or option ARMs).

Negative amortization, which is very undesirable, occurs when unpaid interest is added to your mortgage balance, increasing your future payments. Only consider mortgages with negative amortization features if you are confident that you will be disciplined and able to pay off the loan balance over time.

Question 152: **What are the advantages to using a real estate agent?**

Real estate agents are experts at helping individuals find homes that fit their interests, their budget, and their criteria. They save you time, make your home search more exhaustive and comprehensive, and play on your team. Your agent represents you, and she earns her commission when she finds the home you want at a price you can afford. Your Realtor will negotiate with the seller's broker or the seller, if the owner is selling it on her own, to get the best price possible. And the seller pays her commission!

Question 153: **How do I find a reputable real estate agent?**

Personal recommendations are the best way to find an agent. However, if you're going to a new community, be aware that when you call or walk into a local real estate office, you will likely be assigned to the next agent on rotation—without regard to his experience, qualifications, or work ethic. You can vastly improve your odds by perusing local newspaper ads—real estate brokers reward their top performers by giving them prominent placement in their ads—and then calling someone with a lot of sales under his belt.

Question 154: **What happens when I'm ready to buy?**

Once you've found a dream home you can afford, your agent will contact the seller's agent, who may require "earnest money"—1 to 6 percent of the value of the home in a check or cash—and a contract that indicates the exact amount of your bid and any contingencies. Make sure that the contract gives you a few days to withdraw your bid in case you change your mind. Your "earnest money" will be returned if the deal doesn't go through—usually because you are unable to get the mortgage loan you expected—as long as this is specified in the contract.

Your agent will assist you in offering a realistic bid based on recent sales of homes in the area, one that is adjusted downward from the asking price for extra work required on the home, and upward for special features, like extra bathrooms or a pool.

Question 155: **What are contingencies, and how do they affect a counteroffer?**

The seller may accept your first offer, but typically she will counteroffer, asking for a higher price and/or negotiating the terms—for instance, asking that she be allowed to remain in the home for two months. Negotiations usually go back and forth a few times and will likely take a few days. On your end, your agent can and should include some basic contingencies, as follows:

- Financing
- Inspections
- Closing inspection

Question 156: **What else do I need to know about buying a house?**

One important part of the contract is a written statement that provides full disclosure on the condition of the house—detailing past problems that have been fixed, as well as any issues that have not yet been addressed. In many cases, a seller's failure to offer full disclosure means you have recourse to make him pay for fixing problems after the fact. If you've hired inspectors and studied the full disclosure statement, you will know what you're getting and will be able to judge whether or not it's a good deal.

Also, keep in mind that the costs associated with buying a home—points on your loan, appraisal fees, title fees, up to six months of local real estate tax your lender may require prepaid, inspection fees, document fees, property title transfer fees, and other charges—usually add 3 to 5 percent to the total cost of the home. Your real estate lawyer or lender will be able to give you an estimate of the closing costs you will be required to pay before you submit your offer.

You will also need homeowner's insurance, which lenders usually require to cover your home, personal property, and landscaping from theft, fires, hurricanes, and other calamities.

Question 157: **If I am selling my home, do I need a real estate agent?**

Even though it feels prohibitive, particularly since you will pay the sales commission for your agent and the buyer's agent, when selling an investment as large as your house, it's smart to hire a reputable, aggressive, and professional real estate agent or broker. Whether you love the idea or hate the idea, selling a home is emotional. You need someone with professional savvy who can market your home and negotiate the best deal.

You may be able to negotiate a lower sales percentage with your broker—most agents ask for 6 percent, but you can frequently bargain them down to 5 or even 4 percent (if they get the buyer's agent to agree to trim their take).

Traditionally, the highest-priced offers and the largest volume of offers will come within the first four weeks of listing. Take advantage by sprucing up your home and readying yourself to field offers.

Question 158: **Should I make any improvements before selling my home?**

Ask your agent what you can realistically do to improve the property. Unless absolutely necessary, avoid expensive upgrades. Instead, rent a storage unit and remove all excess clutter, keeping only what makes the home more attractive. Clean the house thoroughly, plant a few flowers, and touch up interior and exterior paint.

If your house needs a new roof or extensive landscaping, tell your agent you are willing to pay for half of a reasonable bid if necessary to make the sale. Faced with the option of living with the cheapest roof or landscaping you can find, the buyer may be willing to negotiate.

On open house days, bake bread or cookies or use scented candles. Soft lighting and classical music also increase ambiance. Home staging companies—which offer interior decoration—are expensive and best left to those with money to burn.

Question 159: **Do I have to be truthful on my "full disclosure" statement?**

Yes—law requires it. If the buyer makes the sale contingent upon your paying for minor repairs, you can usually hire an inexpensive handyman. Failing to disclose latent or unseen problems like seasonal flooding could lead to more expensive repercussions, including expensive lawsuits.

Question 160: **Is it true that I don't have to pay taxes on a huge portion of proceeds?**

When you sell your home, provided you have lived in it for at least two of the past five years, the first $250,000 of gain is not taxed. For instance, if you purchased the home for $150,000, spent $40,000 remodeling it, and sold it for $400,000, your gain—minus the sales commissions and repairs—will fall well under $200,000, which means you will not owe any taxes on the sale.

Question 161: **What do I need to know about buying a car?**

After a home, the next largest purchase you'll make is probably a car. Unlike homes, which generally appreciate in value, cars depreciate, or lose value rapidly. For most of us, buying a car is an unavoidable cost of living.

As with buying a home, shop for the lowest interest rates, and nail down a preapproved loan for an amount you can realistically afford. That way the seller will know that you are serious and that you can pay for the car, which should help you negotiate the best price. Verify the car's value by checking *Kelley Blue Book* (online at *www.kbb.com*) or *www.edmunds.com*.

Question 162: **How do I avoid buying a lemon?**

Most certified car dealers thoroughly check used cars for mechanical issues and offer a guarantee for a certain number of miles and years from the date of your purchase. You may pay more, but the peace of mind can be worth it. *Consumer Reports* publishes an annual *Used Car Buyer's Guide* that provides substantial information on the reliability of different models and model years. If you buy from a private party, hire a qualified mechanic to inspect the car before you buy it. Also, for about $20, check out *www.carfax.com*, *www .autocheck.com*, or *www.cardetective.com*.

Question 163: **Is it better to buy or to lease a car?**

When you purchase a car outright, higher loan payments help you build equity that reduces interest charges; when leasing, you don't build equity and continue to pay interest for the full value of the car. The finance company takes more risk on the value of the vehicle at the end of the lease than it would if it financed your purchase of the vehicle, so you pay more.

In spite of this cautionary advice, if you decide to lease, don't allow low monthly payments to cloud your thinking. Negotiate the purchase price, the interest rate, and the cost of breaking your lease. Also, you'll want "gap coverage" to cover the difference between what your insurance company will pay for "cash value" of the car and what you will owe on the lease if your car is totaled or stolen, as what you owe could be several thousand more than the "cash value."

Chapter 11

PROTECTING YOUR ASSETS

INSURANCE CAN BE costly, and when you're writing a fat check, it can feel like a luxury. However, now that you are making wise investments, paying down your debt, increasing your income, and building a retirement fund, it's time to reassess what you are doing to safeguard those assets. While allowing adept sales pitches to sway your decision is not a good idea, insurance is not a place to slash costs. The educated consumer wants to secure her assets and protect her loved ones without overpaying.

Question 164: **Why do I need insurance?**

It's one thing to generate income and accumulate assets, but it's another to take care of them. You have responsibility to your children—and yourself—to protect your assets. You must read through all the fine print, learn the basics, and then talk to experts who can put the proper insurance protections in place.

If you have a valuable possession, or earn a high income, insurance salespeople will go overboard to sell you multiple policies. While some insurance isn't needed, or simply isn't affordable, you do need some basic types of insurance. The primary ones include these:

- Health and dental insurance
- Life insurance
- Homeowner's or renter's insurance
- Car insurance
- Disability insurance

In an ideal world, you would have maximum insurance coverage. In reality, you may have to make crucial decisions between what you really need and cannot afford to be without and what you can realistically afford.

Question 165: **What are my options when it comes to health and dental insurance?**

Health and dental insurance is an absolute must. Hopefully you, or your children's father, will have coverage through an employer. Working fathers are often required by law to carry their children on their employer's health plan until the children are eighteen, or older if the children attend college full time. If he has this option available, make sure you take advantage of it, and don't be afraid to go to court to do so. It could save you thousands of dollars over the years and guarantee your children the coverage they deserve.

If neither you nor the children's father can acquire health insurance through an employer, you will need to find a plan you can afford that will cover and protect you and your children. In general, your health insurance options are as follows:

- **HMOs:** Health maintenance organizations require a primary care doctor and usually one hospital within their plan.
- **PPOs:** Preferred provider organizations give you a greater range of doctor selection and choices about whether or not you see a specialist or have certain medical tests.
- **Catastrophic coverage:** Premiums are much cheaper, but you will have a high deductible—$2,000, $5,000, or

$10,000—which means you pay everything until the deductible is met.
- **Government assistant plans:** If you have a low income and cannot afford health insurance, you may qualify for state children's health insurance programs (SCHIP) or federal Medicaid assistance. Check out *www.cms.hhs.gov/schip* and *www.insurekidsnow.gov* to see if you qualify.

When it comes to health insurance, it pays to stay current with coverage vernacular and to search for any means of saving money—without sacrificing coverage.

Question 166: **What are flexible spending plans?**

Flexible spending plans are optional plans that employers may be able to offer employees. Basically, you determine a set amount for your employer to withhold from your pretax wages that you can then spend to cover medical and dental costs that your insurance doesn't cover. This saves you 15 to 35 percent a year on co-pays, deductibles, braces, caps, laser eye surgery, over-the-counter medications, and other health care expenses. The only catch is that you have to determine an amount for the entire year.

Question 167: **What are COBRA and HIPAA?**

COBRA is a plan employers are legally required to offer employees who are fired or who leave for any reason, even if it's to transition into part-time work. Employers who employ more than twenty people must offer you (and your children, if they have been covered under the plan) health coverage at their cost, plus 2 percent, for a period of eighteen months. Legally separated, divorced, or widowed spouses are eligible for thirty-six months. However, you must accept the offer within sixty days (thirty days if your spouse died), and don't wait! You won't be able to find independent coverage cheaper, and COBRA protects you, and your children, during transitions.

The Health Insurance Portability and Accountability Act (HIPAA) was created to protect your access to health insurance. Under HIPAA, anyone leaving a group insurance plan is guaranteed coverage as long as you were covered for at least twelve months and switch health care providers within sixty-three days.

Take advantage of COBRA and HIPAA to ensure that you and your children will not be turned down or made to wait for coverage. Allowing a break in insurance gives insurance companies the opportunity to deny coverage, or withhold specific coverage, on the basis of pre-existing conditions.

Question 168: **What are health savings plans?**

If you are self-employed, you can open a health savings account (HSA) that combines high deductible, catastrophic health insurance with a tax-favored savings plan. You make a tax-deductible contribution each year to the HSA to cover medical bills. If you don't use the money, it will accumulate. The maximum amount you can contribute changes annually—currently it's around $5,500 for a family. This option is best for healthy families who have enough money to cover basic medical expenses. Talk to your financial advisor and an insurance broker about whether this plan is a smart move for you.

Question 169: **How can I save money on health insurance?**

There are several ways to save on health insurance, as follows:

- Opt for a large deductible
- Comparison shop
- Review your medical records
- Practice preventive care

Question 170: **What do I need to know about life insurance?**

Most savvy money investors recommend term life insurance for parents. Term means that you pay a set fee per month for a policy that provides a set amount of coverage over ten, twenty, or thirty years. Term insurance is cheaper than whole life, universal life, or variable universal. As long as you choose a term that covers your children's expenses until they become adults, it's sufficient protection.

Question 171: **How much life insurance do I need?**

The Consumer Federation of America recommends that you buy eight times your annual income to cover living expenses for twenty years, or nine times for thirty years. If you want to cover college expenses, add $100,000 per child. Then deduct the value of any life insurance provided by your employer.

If your children's father is carrying life insurance that will adequately safeguard them, you may feel comfortable reducing your life insurance, but make sure you review this with him annually and ask for verification that your children are the beneficiaries of his policy.

Question 172: **How long should I carry life insurance?**

The longer the "term" (five, ten, fifteen, twenty, or thirty years), the higher the monthly premium, but it's wise to weigh whether a slight premium increase is well worth the extra coverage. If you're in your twenties or thirties and your children are toddlers, definitely opt for a thirty-year term. If you're in your forties and your children are in elementary school, the twenty-year term may be sufficient. Ideally, you want coverage either until you reach retirement or until your children are earning a decent income. If you've invested well, your retirement fund should replace the need for life insurance upon retirement.

Question 173: **How can I keep costs to a minimum?**

Insurance companies typically offer volume discounts—lower prices per $1,000 once you exceed a certain level of coverage. Price breaks usually occur in $250,000 increments. If you fall between a break, and if you can afford the higher cost, opt for the higher amount.

Prices can vary widely. The young and healthy win the lowest rates, but no matter your age, it's wise to comparison shop on the Internet. Another thing you can do to lower costs is to keep your credit report clean.

Also, if your employer offers free "portable" (so you can take it if you leave) or "convertible to cash" life insurance, take it and then supplement it with another policy. If the employer's life insurance isn't free, and you're relatively young, you may score lower rates on your own.

Question 174: **How can I make sure I safeguard my home?**

For home insurance, you want a "replacement-cost" policy that will cover the costs of rebuilding your house if it burns to the ground. Don't buy "resale price" coverage—it includes the value of your land, which will not be damaged in a fire. Make sure the face value of the policy increases every year to cover inflationary costs, and consider "extended" or "guaranteed" coverage to cover 25 percent more than the policy's face value.

Question 175: **How do I know which numbers cover what's in my car insurance policy?**

All those paired up numbers can be confusing. Here's a brief run-down of what they mean and what you do and don't need:

- **Liability and property damage coverage:** This covers injuries or damage you cause to other drivers, passengers, pedestrians, and property.

- **Medical:** If you have sufficient health insurance, you don't need this. Opt for zero or minimal coverage.
- **Collision and comprehensive:** Collision covers the cost of damage to your car if you cause an accident, and comprehensive covers random damage or theft.
- **Uninsured or underinsured motorist:** This covers your expenses if someone without any or sufficient insurance hits you.

It makes far more sense to raise your deductibles to keep premiums low than it does to minimize the levels of coverage. Your chances of not needing the coverage are greater than what it will cost you if you do.

Question 176: **What can I do to keep my car insurance rates low?**

If you have an excellent driving record, you may qualify for the lowest rates available. Amica (800-992-6422) offers low car insurance premiums to safe drivers, but you have to meet their rigid standards to qualify. Also, anyone with military experience, or who has a family member (parent or spouse) who served in the military, is eligible for reduced rates through USAA (*www.usaa.com*). Another option is to minimize coverage, but there are smarter (and safer) ways to lower your car insurance premiums:

- Drive safely
- Contest traffic tickets
- Pay all fines promptly
- Take a defensive driving course
- Check your policy annually.
- Lower your mileage
- Avoid SUVs
- Drive cheap cars

Finally, always remember to ask about discounts. Not smoking; having a clean driving record; using antitheft devices; installing anti-lock brakes; automatic seatbelts and airbags; and having good grades or not using a cell phone in the car can all lower your rates—but you have to ask!

Question 177: **How do I research insurance options?**

Even the cost of basic insurance can vary widely. Consumer surveys have found insurers who will inflate their insurance policy rates at a price 400 percent higher than their competitors. You can save a lot of dough just by shopping around and knowing what's within reason.

Explore policy and cost options on the Internet (*www.insure .com* or *www.accuquote.com*); or call Termquote (800-444-8376) or Quotesmith (800-556-9393) for multiple comparisons; or find a local independent broker who isn't locked into one company.

Question 178: **How do I find a reputable insurance broker?**

The best way to find a reputable broker is to ask people in your community—coworkers, church members, friends, family. You can also call your local chamber of commerce and the Better Business Bureau to see if anyone has filed complaints. Having a one-on-one relationship with a good broker can be profitable and rewarding for you both. A reputable, smart broker will help you make decisions that benefit you and your children. Take the time necessary to make sure you're working with someone you trust, and when you find him or her, consider placing all of your policies under one umbrella.

Question 179: **What do I need to do to make sure my children are protected?**

When you are responsible for children under the age of eighteen, two of the most important decisions you make are these:

- Who is the beneficiary of my insurance policies and retirement plans?
- Who do I want to take care of my children in the event of my death?

Anyone you name as a beneficiary on insurance policies or retirement plans will remain the beneficiary, no matter what you express verbally or even what you record in a formal will. It's vital to review your choices every five years, or whenever your circumstances change, to make sure you have the names and the proportions the way you want them.

If you have minor children, when it comes to naming a guardian or guardians, there are two primary questions you need to answer:

- Who will take day-to-day physical custody of my children?
- Who will manage their money and property (including insurance proceeds)?

Often, one person will fulfill both of these roles, but if not, you need to specify the delineation in your will. Also, you may not want your children to assume control of the money and property at age eighteen, in which case you may want to create a trust that oversees the financial aspects until they finish college or reach milestones, such as age twenty-one or twenty-five.

In most cases, the remaining parent assumes custody of the minor children, but you can establish a guardian for their financial and property inheritance. You may also want to name a guardian in case your ex-husband dies before the children reach eighteen. If you do not want the children's father to gain full custody, you can name a guardian and then write a letter explicitly stating your reasons for doing so. In the event of your death, the court would review the documents and make a decision about whether your children would be better off under the care of your named guardian. If you are adamant that your children's legal father should not have custody, consult a lawyer.

Question 180: **Even if I don't have many assets, do I need a will?**

If you have dependent children, creating a legal will is essential. Not only do you need to provide for their financial welfare, you need to designate guardians. Avoid any ideas of hastily writing down instructions and presuming it becomes a legal will. State laws vary, and what you think will suffice very often absolutely will not. Wills have to go through probate court. The simpler you keep the will, the less it will cost to distribute your assets to your heirs, but having a legal will drawn up by a lawyer will keep the cost of probate lower and better serve your intentions.

Laws vary state by state. If you're going to draw up a will yourself, make sure you know the laws in your state and abide by them. In general, wills have to be neither notarized, nor submitted to the court, nor stamped with any legal imprint prior to your death. In some states, however, anyone who signs your will as a witness cannot inherit anything, despite what your will says. Also, handwritten wills are legal in some states but not in others. Unless they are properly witnessed (the rules for which differ by state), typewritten wills are usually tossed out, and videotaped wills are invalid in most states.

Question 181: **What is a living trust?**

A living trust is a document that assigns a trustee to handle your estate in the event of your death. It's essentially a will that doesn't have to go through probate. You create a list of your beneficiaries, the name of a guardian or guardians, and how you wish matters to be handled. You then draw up a living trust that allows your designated trustee to distribute your estate according to your wishes. A living trust makes more sense if you own a business or have complicated real estate holdings.

Question 182: **What do I do if I want to create a will or a living trust?**

Neither a will nor a living trust has to be complicated. In both cases, the most important information you need to gather is the following:

- A list of all your assets
- A list of all your liabilities
- A list of beneficiaries
- Guardian(s)
- Trustee(s)
- Executor(s)

It's your job as a single mother to make crucial decisions that directly affect your children's welfare. In the event no will has been created, a legal system that may, or may not, make the best decisions will be in charge of your estate. Spare your children. Do all the research required, and then create a will or a living trust that will safeguard their future.

Question 183: **What is a living will?**

A living will, also called a health care directive, is a legal document that directs doctors and your family what to do if you are permanently unconscious, irreversibly brain damaged, suffering from dementia, or dying and unable to speak or make decisions. While it seems gruesome, imagine how your children would feel if they were ever asked to make a decision about whether you lived or died. Spare them the anguish and make these decisions for yourself.

Also, it's wise to name a health care proxy or assign "durable power of attorney" to someone you trust to give and receive medical information and enforce your living will.

You can find forms on the Internet or in books that will help you sort out all the issues and make firm decisions. Do this when you are formulating a will and save money by having your lawyer draw up the documents at the same time.

Question 184: **Do I have to legally file my will?**

Wills do not have to be officially recorded or filed in a court, which means it's up to you to keep yours in a safe place. If you keep all your important papers, such as insurance policies, birth certificates, mortgage papers, house deed, and your will in a safe deposit box, make sure your executor has access to it. It's perhaps wiser to keep them in a waterproof and fireproof box at your home, as long as the executor knows where to find it. It's also wise to include all papers that would assist in handling your estate—a list of all credit card numbers, bank accounts, retirement funds, insurance policies, and creditors. Make it a habit to review these documents annually and update information so that you'll have everything in order in case of an emergency.

Chapter **12**

FUNDING COLLEGE

IN THE LAST ten years, public and private four-year college costs increased about 2.5 and 2 percent, respectively, above the rate of inflation. If this trend continues, in ten years you can expect that college costs will increase 5 to 7 percent per year—totaling about $50,000 per year for the average private four-year college; $22,000 per year for the average public four-year college; and $14,500 per year for the average two-year college. So, if you want to pay a large part of your children's college expenses, the earlier you start planning, saving, and investing, the better.

Question 185: **What is the best way to approach paying for college?**

The two best ways to save for your child's education are to open a Coverdell education savings account and/or a section 529 college savings plan. Their basic allowances and qualifications are as follows:

- You can contribute $2,000 each year to a Coverdell account. Money in the account grows tax-free, and it can be spent on almost any education-related expense for your child as soon as he or she starts first grade.

■ You can deposit significantly larger annual amounts in 529 plans earmarked for college expenses. The plans allow new contributions until the account value reaches a certain level that varies by state—most of the lowest limits max out at $235,000; the higher limits max out around $300,000. To retain tax-free status on gains, you must spend withdrawn money on tuition, room and board, fees, books, supplies, and equipment used for college and graduate school—not for any earlier education expenses.

■ You can deposit money into a section 529 plan that allows you to prepurchase four years of tuition at today's prices at one of your state's public universities or one of a number of private schools. Deposits are limited to the cost of tuition and required fees for five years.

Question 186: **So how do Coverdell Education Savings Accounts work?**

If your 2006 modified adjusted gross income (MAGI) is less than $110,000, you can contribute a maximum of $2,000 per year, per child, to a Coverdell account in a given child's name. Total annual contributions per child can be as much as $2,000 from all parties contributing. The minor can also fund his or her own account, but the total from all sources per year cannot exceed $2,000. Gains and interest on investments in the account grow tax-free for the life of the account. You won't be taxed on withdrawals at the federal level (or, in most cases, by the state) as long as the money is spent on qualifying educational expenses for things required for your child's education from the day your child starts first grade.

Question 187: **What are the advantages and disadvantages of a Coverdell account?**

If you withdraw money from a Coverdell account that you don't spend on qualified education expenses, you will have to pay ordinary income tax at a relatively high rate on a pro-rata share of earnings on the withdrawal, as well as a 10 percent penalty on the same withdrawn earnings. For instance, if you withdraw $1,000 from an account with a total value of $10,000 and account gains of $5,000, you would owe taxes and penalties on $500 of gains. The only real drawback to a Coverdell account is that you can only contribute $2,000 a year. Thankfully, you have other options that you can choose instead of—or in addition to—a Coverdell account. There are many advantages and disadvantages to these accounts and they really depend on your situation. Check out the Internet or talk to your financial planner about what Coverdell can mean for you.

Question 188: **How do Section 529 college savings plans work?**

Since 1996, parents have had a choice between two kinds of 529 college savings plans to pay for their children's education. You can establish a 529 plan that will function as an investment account in which gains and interest aren't taxed, or you can establish a 529 prepaid tuition plan, which allows you to purchase blocks of college tuition (by semester) for your child at today's prices. Both types of 529 plans offer excellent savings opportunities and share common features.

Both plans generate from either an individual state or educational institution. States and educational institutions are the only groups allowed to create 529 plans. Plan management is often delegated to a major financial firm like T Rowe Price, Fidelity, or Vanguard; however many states run their own programs. Each plan is unique in terms of the investments it allows as well as its various restrictions and fees. To make the right decision for your situation, get the "offering circular" from the plan sponsor and thoroughly review plan details before you open the account.

Question 189: **What's involved in managing a 529 plan?**

The function of a 529 plan is similar to that of a Roth IRA. Your deposits are not deducted from your gross income on your tax return; however, you may receive modest state tax credits or deductions in a given year. The money you deposit into your 529 plan is limited to one or a few investment options offered by the plan—usually stock and bond mutual funds—and your savings grow tax-free until you're ready to withdraw them to cover qualified educational expenses. If you choose an investment-type 529 plan, you have the potential to earn a higher return than you would with a prepaid tuition plan; however, you also take on stock and bond market risk in the process.

You can avoid paying taxes and penalties on earnings in your 529 savings by spending the account's assets on qualified higher education expenses (QHEE), including college and graduate school tuition, room and board, mandatory fees, books, supplies, and even computers or other equipment required by the school. The school receiving the money must also be eligible to disburse federal financial aid. (See *www.fafsa.ed.gov* for a list of qualified schools.) The list includes overseas, technical, and trade schools, as well as traditional universities and junior colleges.

For federal financial aid purposes, 529 plans are treated as assets of the parent rather than the child. This means your child has increased ability to receive financial aid when she has a certain amount of money in a 529 plan than she does with the same amount in a custodial account in her own name. Also, even after the child reaches age eighteen or twenty-one, you maintain control of the account. You can withdraw money not spent on education by paying a 10-percent penalty and taxes on the profits accrued.

If you withdraw money from both a 529 plan and a Coverdell account in the same year, you have to split your qualified higher education expenses (QHEE) between the accounts to determine whether any taxes are due. If you spend $5,000 on tuition and other QHEE during a year, the total amount of QHEE you can cover between the two accounts is $5,000; no double counting is allowed.

Question 190: **How do 529 prepaid tuition plans work?**

The 529 prepaid tuition plan allows you to purchase tuition credits at any school that has signed up to take part in your state's plan. Because tuition has risen much faster than inflation for decades, this can be an attractive way to finance your child's education, but there are caveats.

Generally, your child cashes in the credits by attending a school in the plan (in most cases, a state university), and tuition (and in some cases room and board) is paid by the plan. If your child wants to attend a college not covered by the plan, the plan usually pays the value of your child's tuition credits directly to the other institution. If that institution has lower tuition and fees than state schools, the plan will usually pay the lower amount. Since you may sacrifice money in this situation, you should evaluate whether the best option is simply to cancel the contract and get a refund.

Seemingly, prepaid tuition guarantees that your child will be able to afford tuition and fees at the preferred state school and limits investment risk; however, when their prepayment investments didn't grow at the same rate as college-cost inflation (5 to 7 percent annually), or their plan didn't attract a critical asset mass to make it self-sufficient, a few states canceled their contracts, which left investors to find an alternative plan in another state.

Question 191: **How can I make sure the plan will still be available when my child is ready?**

To avoid investing in 529 prepaid tuition plans that are in danger of folding, look for a plan that has many other investors and a large amount of assets. Check out the College Savings Plans Network's "Statistics Warehouse" website (online at *www.collegesavings.org*), as well as the website *www.savingforcollege.com*. Both include side-by-side state-sponsored 529 plan comparisons, which are excellent starting points for further research.

Question 192: **What other options are available?**

Educational savings bonds are a safe, tax-advantaged option, but they typically don't accrue enough interest to bolster savings. Custodial accounts are an option; however, they don't offer tax advantages and can be problematic if your children get ownership at age eighteen or twenty-one and squander the money. Using your Roth IRA to fund your child's education is also possible, and it may be reasonable if you are at least age 59.5 when your child attends college. Still, this approach isn't generally recommended because withdrawals from the account are counted by financial aid formulas as parental income and could limit access to additional financial aid. Also, using your Roth IRA may create a situation in which you have to choose between your retirement savings and your child's education.

Question 193: **How do custodial accounts work?**

Established in some states under the Uniform Gifts to Minors Act (UGMA), and in others as the Uniform Transfers to Minors Act (UTMA), parents or guardians are allowed to establish custodial accounts. These are simple trust accounts opened for someone under twenty-one years of age and controlled by the custodian, usually one of the account holder's parents, until the child reaches adulthood. A deposit into a child's custodial account is considered a gift to your child; however, you, as the custodian, are responsible for managing the account assets until your child reaches age eighteen or twenty-one, depending on the state you live in. Currently, you are allowed to make a gift of $12,000 tax-free per year. When your child reaches the relevant age, he owns the account, and you will no longer have legal control over how he chooses to spend the money you intended for college. Once you make a gift of the money, it cannot be reclaimed, even if you find yourself in dire financial straits.

Question 194: **Will my child have to pay taxes on her custodial account?**

A child under age fourteen will earn tax-free gains on the first $850 in investment income (interest, dividends, and capital gains), and pay taxes at her marginal tax rate for the next $850 of investment income. Any investment income in her custodial account over $1,700 will be taxed at your marginal tax rate. After age fifteen, all gains in the account will be taxable at her tax rate.

Question 195: **Wouldn't it be better to opt for tax-advantaged accounts?**

Yes, it's best to use tax-advantaged account options like a 529 savings plan to fund your child's college expenses rather than a custodial account for three reasons:

1. If your child has a custodial account, the account will reduce his available federal financial aid by 3.5 times (in 2007) more than the amount that it would be reduced if he had the same amount of money in a 529 plan.
2. Custodial accounts owe taxes on all realized gains; 529 account earnings are not taxed.
3. No matter your child's age, you maintain control of 529 plan assets.

Even at age eighteen or twenty-one, children are not likely to understand the financial sacrifices you made to accumulate college funds or to spend them wisely. To avoid disappointment, it's advisable to choose plans that remain under your control.

Question 196: **What about education savings bonds?**

You can also purchase government-backed bonds—Series EE and Series I bonds—that earn tax-free interest income as long as the bonds are eventually used to pay for qualifying college and graduate school expenses. The U.S. government guarantees both bond types, so you have almost no risk of losing money; however, interest rates will be lower than most investment alternatives. Qualified college and graduate school expenses include tuition and mandatory fees for a degree-granting college or graduate school, or any school eligible to disburse federal financial aid (see *www.fafsa.ed.gov* for a list of qualified schools).

Series I bonds increase in value based on the level of inflation measured by the Consumer Price Index (CPI), plus a return over inflation, while Series EE bonds are guaranteed to at least double in value within twenty years—which equates to a 3.5-percent minimum annual return.

Question 197: **How do I purchase education savings bonds?**

To purchase these bonds and take full advantage of the federal tax breaks, you must be at least twenty-four years old and have a modified adjusted gross income (MAGI) below $63,100 (for 2006). If your MAGI falls between $63,100 and $78,100 when you cash in the bonds, you will receive a partial federal tax deduction. You can purchase up to $30,000 of each kind of education savings bond each year. They can be purchased through most brokerage firms or direct from the U.S. Treasury Department (online at *www .treasurydirect.gov*) in denominations as low as $25.

Local and state governments do not impose tax on education savings bond gains. You are required to hold Series I and EE bonds for at least twelve months. If for any reason you sell the bonds within five years of original purchase, you will lose the most recent three months' interest paid on the bonds. Finally, education savings bonds can be transferred tax-free into a 529 savings plan, but you still forfeit the most recent three months' interest if you redeem the bonds within five years of their purchase.

Question 198: **Is there a way to circumvent having the bonds negatively affect financial aid?**

To avoid limiting your child's access to financial aid, buy the bonds in your name, and hold them until the year you begin paying for her college or graduate school expenses. If you spend less than the full amount of the Series I and EE bonds you sell in a given year on qualified expenses, you'll have to pay taxes on the remainder of your gains.

Question 199: **How do education reward programs work?**

Some credit cards offer education reward programs that work in the same way as money-back, store-credit, or airline-miles programs. When you purchase goods or services from businesses partnered with the rewards program, they typically deposit 1 to 5 percent of the purchase into your child's 529 account. You can also sign up friends, family, godparents, and others naming your child the rewards beneficiary, which can potentially increase your child's college savings by thousands of dollars over the years.

Question 200: **What is the Hope Credit?**

The Hope Credit is a nonrefundable credit that can be used to offset taxes you owe for qualified expenses up to $1,000, plus half of expenses over $1,000, with a maximum credit amount of $1,500. Qualified expenses include tuition and required fees for you or your dependent to attend the first two years of a qualified postsecondary school (eligible to disburse federal financial aid) and required books or supplies purchased directly from the college or school.

To calculate how much your credit will be reduced or find more information about the Hope Credit, consult IRS Publication 970, or visit the IRS website, at *www.irs.gov*.

Question 201: **Would we also be able to claim the Lifetime Learning Credit?**

Education expenses that qualify for the Hope Credit also qualify for the Lifetime Learning Credit; however, the credit is not restricted to the first two years of the student's higher education. The two credits have the same key qualifying income levels as well. The credit is for 20 percent of up to $10,000 of qualifying expenses per family tax return, up to a maximum of $2,000 that may be attributable to qualifying expenses from more than one child in the family.

You cannot claim the Hope Credit and the Lifetime Learning Credit in the same year. But if you have more than one student in the family (including yourself), you could use the Hope Credit for one and the Lifetime Learning Credit for the other if your child or you are in the first two years of college, and if the relevant qualifying expenses are under $7,500 for the calendar year. If you have to decide between the Lifetime Learning Credit and the Hope Credit, given current tax law, the Hope Credit offers greater financial rewards. If qualified expenses paid are over $7,500, the higher-limit Lifetime Learning Credit ($2,000 maximum) is the better choice.

Question 202: **How do federal student aid programs work?**

About 60 percent of undergraduates enrolled full-time in college receive federal, state, or school grant aid. If you pay interest on a nonfederal loan that you are liable for, you are able to deduct the interest on your taxes. Scholarship money used for tuition and course-related expenses are tax-free; however, money used to pay room and board is taxable.

For all federal aid programs, your student must file the Free Application for Federal Student Aid (FAFSA) each year. The FAFSA filing establishes the expected family contribution (EFC) for your child, a figure used commonly in federal financial aid calculations. You can file the FAFSA either online (*www.fafsa.ed.gov*)

or by submitting a paper form that you can get from your local high school or college.

A variety of federal student aid programs exist, as described in the following sections.

Question 203: **How do Pell grants work?**

Since they are outright subsidies that do not have to be repaid, Pell grants are the most popular form of student aid—traditionally claimed by approximately 5 million students each year. Pell grant awards are based on the cost of attending the specific school and the student's EFC. For the 2006–2007 school year, the EFC cutoff is $3,851. (When the EFC is greater than this figure, the student is ineligible.) Grants can go as high as $4,050 each year to qualifying students. The U.S. Department of Education posts an annual grant eligibility form on the department's website at *http://studentaid.ed.gov.*

Question 204: **How do Supplemental Education Opportunity Grants work?**

Families with low EFCs are eligible to claim a Supplemental Education Opportunity Grant (SEOG) as additional support for college expenses. SEOG awards can also reach $4,000 per year and do not have to be repaid. Schools typically grant these awards on a first-come, first-served basis, so submitting applications as soon as possible is crucial to getting support. According to guidance from the U.S. Department of Education, Pell grant–eligible students with the lowest EFC are the first to receive these grants. The next group to receive funds is non-Pell students who have the lowest EFCs.

Question 205: **How do Stafford loans work?**

If a student has demonstrable financial need (as documented on her FAFSA) and is enrolled at least half-time, he may qualify for a low-interest Stafford loan. Undergraduate students who are someone's dependent for financial aid purposes are able to borrow progressively larger amounts—in 2006, loan amounts were $2,625 in the student's first year, $3,500 in the second year, and $5,500 for each of the third and fourth years. Undergraduate students who aren't someone's dependent can borrow up to $6,625 in their first year, $7,500 in their second, and $10,500 in their third and fourth years; however, the federally subsidized portions of these loans are offered only up to the maximums for dependent students. Post-graduate and professional students (such as those at medical or law school) can receive $18,500 in loans for each year of study, but no more than $8,500 can be subsidized.

There are two varieties of Stafford loans. Banks, credit unions, or other traditional lenders provide Federal Family Education Loans (FFEL), and the U.S. Department of Education offers Direct Stafford Loans. FFEL loans must be repaid by between ten and twenty-five years after graduation; Direct Stafford Loan recipients must repay between ten to thirty years after graduation.

Question 206: **How do PLUS loans work?**

Parent Loans for Undergraduate Students (PLUS) are available to families (including the parent of the dependent child) that pass a credit check. Your school may offer two kinds of PLUS package: Direct PLUS loans are offered by the U.S. Department of Education, and FFEL PLUS loans are offered by nongovernment lenders. FFEL PLUS loans are offered to parents of dependent undergraduate students enrolled at least half time, up to a maximum of the total cost of attendance, less other financial aid received. Interest rates are low and change every year. You'll have between ten and twenty-five years to repay loans outstanding on a FFEL PLUS loan.

Direct PLUS loans are offered with the same requirements as FFEL PLUS loans; however, FFEL PLUS loans allow repayment based on the amount of income you earn. Families can select an "income-sensitive" repayment plan with higher payments when family income is higher and lower payments when income is less.

Question 207: **How do Perkins loans work?**

Undergraduate and graduate-level students with "exceptional" financial need, as defined by the college, can get federal Perkins loans, which have interest rates that hold steady at 5 percent. Eligible undergraduate students can borrow up to $4,000 per year through the program, or up to $20,000 total. Graduate students can borrow up to $6,000 per year, up to a maximum of $40,000, including undergraduate loans outstanding under the program. Graduates have a nine-month grace period and then ten years to pay off the loan. Your school will likely disburse Perkins loans on a first-come, first-served basis, so it's imperative that students apply as soon as possible.

Question 208: **How do federal work-study programs work?**

The federal work-study program offers part-time employment to students with financial need to offset their college expenses. Usually students work directly for their college, fulfilling a variety of roles, but they may also work for an unrelated public agency or private nonprofit organization. In limited cases, they are able to work with private, for-profit employers when the job is relevant to the student's course of study.

Question 209: **Are there any other options for funding college?**

The most important, and incidentally least expensive, way for you to help prepare your child for college is to stress the importance of your child's excelling academically, athletically, or in other activities she enjoys (all of which will help her win scholarships and grants). Encourage your child's development, teach her that college will help her achieve whatever she desires, and cultivate the idea of college as a necessary rite of passage to adulthood. If you do this, she may become motivated to work harder in high school, to work harder to help raise money for her college education, and to make sacrifices that will allow you to channel additional money into her college funds.

If you cannot adequately fund college savings plans, make sure your child's father contributes at least as much as you do. Devote at least a small percentage of child support to fund the account, and ask your family to donate 20 to 25 percent or more of what they would spend on gifts for the children to their college funds. It's also completely reasonable to reward your children with deposits into their account every time they bring home a good report card, or to offer to match whatever savings they are willing to contribute. These days it takes commitment and discipline to save enough to send your children to college. Consider it a noble sacrifice, research your options, and be inventive.

Chapter **13**

FUNDING YOUR RETIREMENT

EVEN IF RETIREMENT seems like a distant star, planning for retirement has become an issue that few can afford to ignore. Government programs—Social Security, Medicare, and Medicaid—that have traditionally supplemented retirement are rapidly diminishing. Few will receive enough government support to live a comfortable lifestyle, much less take care of their basic needs, including health care. As a single mother, the responsibility to plan for your retirement falls squarely upon your shoulders. The sooner you face reality and begin, the better you will fare in your twilight years.

Question 210: **How can I secure my retirement?**

The only way to secure your future is to implement a savings plan designated for retirement funds. If your employer offers a retirement plan, jump in with both feet. If not, by all means, open individual retirement accounts (IRAs) and make a commitment to fund them to the maximum amount allowed per year, or at least the maximum you can reasonably afford. You cannot afford to limp along—saving some months, and depleting your savings in others. If you are not contributing regularly to your retirement savings, you need to take control of your spending habits now.

Question 211: **How do employer-sponsored defined contribution retirement plans work?**

The majority of American companies still offer "defined contribution retirement plans" for their employees. But in this era of cutbacks and downsizing, some companies have started diminishing, or even completely eradicating, retirement benefit plans. So, if you are lucky enough to work for an employer that offers retirement benefits, especially if it offers to match whatever money you contribute, celebrate your good fortune and pony up as much cash as you can. And when you change jobs, DO NOT cash in your retirement fund. We'll discuss how to transfer it into another retirement account later. The important thing to know is that this is one financial decision that carries real weight.

Question 212: **What's the difference between 401(k) and 403(b) plans?**

401(k) and 403(b) plans are employer-sponsored savings plans that allow you to save current income without paying current taxes on the savings. Private companies offer 401(k) plans; and 403(b) plans are offered by public, educational, and nonprofit organizations. The 403(b) plans are tax-sheltered retirement plans with distinct differences from 401(k) plans. These 403(b) specialized plans are offered to teachers, hospital workers, and employees of nonprofit organizations. Also, to keep plan costs low, 403(b) plans may offer investment options limited to fixed and variable annuities. Employers typically offer 401(k) and 403(b) retirement plans as an employee benefit.

Question 213: **What are the advantages of 401(k) and 403(b) plans?**

These company-sponsored retirement plans have additional very attractive features:

- Employers can use direct deposit for all contributions—what you don't see, you don't miss, and can't spend.
- Unless you owe money to the IRS, or to an ex-spouse as part of a court-brokered divorce settlement, your creditors generally cannot touch your 401(k) funds if you declare personal bankruptcy.
- You may be able to borrow money from the plan, allowing you to access the plan's value before retirement (borrowing from retirement plans will discussed in depth later in this chapter).

Question 214: **What are the disadvantages or limitations of 401(k) and 403(b) plans?**

Although they are largely good, 401(k) and 403(b) plans do have some limitations. For example, your 401(k) plan may charge administration fees on top of the fees levied by the mutual funds offered within the plan (usually less than 1 percent of your assets), which will reduce your financial returns. Plans with fewer than 100 participants may be assessed "wrap fees," which at the high end can reach 1.5 percent of assets per year—compromising your ability to grow your retirement assets.

Also, your employer may not make its matching contributions until the end of the relevant year's tax-filing deadline, which means you may wait for matching contributions until the second half of the year following the year you made the related contribution. The sooner the money is deposited, the sooner you begin earning additional money.

Also, 401(k) plans are limited by the documents your employer created to govern the plan. Limitations may include your inability to borrow against your account and trade individual stocks and bonds. You can lobby your employer to change the plan's features, but your employer controls the outcome of requests for change.

Question 215: **How do vesting periods work?**

Your 401(k) or 403(b) plan will come with a vesting period, which is the time period over which you earn ownership to the matching contributions your employer has made to the account. Any money you contribute is automatically yours. There are two types of vesting periods. "Cliff vesting" means you receive full ownership of matching contributions at one time; "graduated vesting" gives you ownership of a certain percent of matching contributions each year.

Typically, graduated vesting means that you acquire ownership in incremental percentages according to the length of employment. Laws regulate the minimum amount of vesting of matching contributions: Cliff vesting must happen within three years of the matching contribution, and graduated vesting must start within two years and be complete within six years.

Question 216: **What's the difference between nonmatching and matching contributions?**

Some employers offer "nonmatching contributions," which means that they establish a set amount of money, usually as a percentage of your salary that the employer will deposit into your 401(k) or 403(b) retirement plan each year. Your employer would pay nonmatching contributions whether or not you contributed to your own 401(k) plan. Nonmatching contributions usually take longer to vest—a maximum of five years for cliff vesting plans, and a maximum of seven years for graduated vesting plans.

If your employer offers matching contributions to your 401(k) plan—paying a certain amount into the plan when you contribute—by all means make maximum use of the offer, and continue to deposit beyond the matching number if at all possible. There are few, if any, other safe, easy, and legal ways to earn 10 to 100 percent (depending on the generosity of your employer) on your money.

Question 217: **Is there a maximum amount I can contribute?**

The maximum amount you can contribute to your 401(k) plan is 15 percent of your annual salary until it reaches a certain number. In 2006, the maximum allowable for employees age forty-nine years and younger was $15,000, and $20,000 for employees fifty or older. Maximums are adjusted for inflation so should be reviewed annually. If your employer makes a contribution to your 401(k), that amount is not added to your contribution when calculating your maximum annual limit, so by all means, contribute as much as you can afford until you reach the limit. Retirement plans are one place where maxing out your options is one of the smartest financial decisions you can make.

Question 218: **Is it ever smart to borrow from my 401(k) retirement plan?**

Rarely. Here's how it works: Many 401(k) plans allow loans, limited by law to a maximum of 50 percent of the employee's vested balance or $50,000—whichever is lower. Loans must be repaid within five years, usually in equal monthly payments, unless they are for the purchase of your primary residence. If you borrow to buy your primary residence, you may benefit from relatively low loan rates. However, you won't benefit from the tax deductibility of interest on a traditional home loan, and you usually have to repay the loan within twenty-five years.

As long as you can afford payments, this money could be used to pay off expensive short-term debts, but you will pay a one-time fee when the loan is made (usually about $50), and may pay annual service fees (also around $50). Interest rates are usually "prime rate" plus 1 percent, with payments deducted from your paycheck. If you leave, or are fired by your employer, you will have to pay off the loan. If you aren't able to fully pay off the loan, remaining balances will be treated as an early withdrawal from your 401(k), meaning you will pay "ordinary income" taxes and a 10-percent early withdrawal penalty unless you are over age 59.5. Interest on the loan is payable to your account, but you may earn less on your own payments than you would if the money remained invested in stock and bonds.

So basically, never borrow from your 401(k) unless you have a genuine, pressing need and no other resources.

Question 219: **What are defined benefit plans?**

A defined benefit plan guarantees employees a certain payment schedule when they retire.

Defined benefit payouts usually increase steadily based on the time you've served with the firm and your average, or highest, salary over your last few of years of employment. Most plans offer incentives for employees to work until age sixty-five, and those who don't have reduced payments for the life of the support.

If you are eligible for a defined benefit plan, it's important to know its vesting schedule. Similar to some tax-advantaged accounts, defined benefit plans have either cliff vesting schedules, which allow you ownership of a certain level of benefits at one time, or graduated vesting, which awards you ownership of the plan's benefits gradually over time. If you change jobs or are fired before some or all of your benefits are fully vested, you will lose any claim to the nonvested benefits.

If your firm offers a defined benefit plan, seek out a human resources person at your firm and ask for clarification on what the specific benefits are and how quickly you become vested. Make sure you know the consequences of changing jobs or losing employment. If you receive an attractive job offer at another firm, make sure you weigh the new retirement plan against the benefits of your current defined benefits plan. Sometimes the defined benefits plan offers "assets" that far outweigh an increased salary being offered elsewhere.

Question 220: **What are profit-sharing plans?**

Profit-sharing plans are usually offered along with a 401(k) and allow contributions only from employers. Your employer may contribute between 0 and 25 percent of your income each year to the plan, to a maximum of $44,000 in 2006 (adjusted annually for inflation), with benefits beginning to accrue no later than two years into your employment. Vesting restrictions apply, with the most common vesting schedule being 20 percent per year starting in the second year of employment. Investment earnings grow with taxes deferred until you withdraw money. You'll be charged a 10 percent penalty for withdrawals from a profit-sharing plan before you reach age 59.5. There are two main differences between this type of plan and a 401(k). The maximum you're allowed to put into profit-sharing, tax-advantaged retirement accounts in total is higher, and profit-sharing plans can have longer vesting periods, up to seven years. They both grow tax-free and are taxed as ordinary income when you withdraw funds from the plan.

Question 221: **What are Employee Stock Ownership Plans (ESOPs)?**

With an Employee Stock Ownership Plan, your employer puts shares of company stock into the account. You can become rich through an ESOP if your company's stock does well over time, but you'll also usually end up with an extra-large position in your own company's stock. You have no control over the shares in an ESOP until you've been with the company for a while, usually ten years, and are over age fifty-five. If you've been part of the plan for at least ten years, at fifty-five, you have the option to sell 25 percent of your holdings, and at sixty, you can sell a total of 50 percent for diversification purposes. Contributions aren't counted as income in the year made, and plan assets grow tax-free until you withdraw funds. Tax treatment of withdrawals is complex, so seek help from a tax professional.

Question 222: **What are individual retirement plans?**

Individual retirement plans allow any income-earning citizen to start a tax-advantaged retirement account with many of the same benefits and drawbacks as company-sponsored retirement plans. Whether or not you're covered by a defined benefit plan, or by another plan that relies on the trustworthiness of many different managers at your company, individual retirement accounts are a great way to build a separate investment account that puts you in the driver's seat.

Unlike employer-sponsored plans, you are responsible for opening a traditional individual retirement account (IRA) and making annual contributions. Contributions reduce your gross taxable income, and IRA investments grow tax-free until withdrawn, at which point they are taxed as ordinary income. As with 401(k) and related plans, in the event you file for bankruptcy, your IRA assets should be protected from seizure.

Question 223: **How much can I contribute to my IRA each year?**

Contributions to your IRA can be as high as 100 percent of your gross income, not including investment gains and dividends, up to $5,000 per year if you're under fifty years old, and $6,000 per year if older. If you have more than one traditional IRA, these limits apply to the total contributions you make in a given year to the accounts. Contributions can be made to your IRA at any time during the related year through the date for filing your tax return for the year, excluding extensions. The date changes, so always check when your contribution is due early in the year.

Question 224: **What are qualifications or restrictions unique to an IRA?**

Other IRA qualifications or restrictions include the following:

- If you make more than $110,000, you can't contribute.
- If your modified adjusted gross income is between $95,000 and $110,000 and you file taxes as single, head of household, or married filing separately, and you didn't live with your spouse at any time during the year, your maximum contribution is restricted.
- You cannot borrow money from your IRA, nor can you sell property to an IRA, use the IRA to secure a loan, or use the IRA to purchase property for personal use.
- If you receive an IRA as part of a divorce or separate maintenance decree, the IRA becomes yours, and the transfer is tax-free.
- If you were divorced or legally separated within a year, and didn't remarry before the end of the calendar year (December 31), and you contributed money to your ex-spouse's IRA that year, you cannot deduct any contributions you made to your ex-spouse's IRA.
- If you inherit an IRA from someone who wasn't your spouse, you can't roll the funds over into your own account. You'll be required to withdraw money over time, and withdrawn amounts will be taxed as ordinary income.
- If you change jobs and your new employer doesn't offer a 401(k) retirement plan, you can "roll over" your funds from the previous employee-sponsored retirement plan into a new "rollover IRA."
- As long as you have earned taxable income in a given year, you can continue to contribute to an IRA until you are age 70.5. You can withdraw money from your IRA when you reach age 59.5 without incurring a penalty.
- If you are making your contribution around tax time, it's very important to specify which year the contribution covers.

Question 225: **What is a Roth IRA?**

A Roth IRA has the same basic requirements and restrictions as a traditional IRA, but with some crucial differences. With a traditional IRA, you fund the account with pretax dollars (by deducting the contribution) meaning you pay less in taxes up front. With a Roth IRA, you fund the account with post-tax dollars (by not deducting the contribution), which means you'll pay more in immediate taxes. However, unlike a traditional IRA, you will not pay any taxes on Roth IRA interest earnings or capital gains—as long as you do not withdraw money within five years of depositing it and are over age 59.5 at the time of withdrawal. If you do withdraw money before those requirements have been met, you will be required to pay a 10-percent early withdrawal penalty and taxes on withdrawn gains and any interest income. The benefits increase substantially if you are young and have many years to acquire gains.

Question 226: **What is the difference between traditional and Roth IRAs?**

The amount you can contribute, the early withdrawal penalty, and most other aspects of the Roth IRA are identical to the traditional IRA, with a few exceptions:

- With a traditional IRA, you cannot contribute to IRA accounts past age 70.5; with a Roth IRA, you can continue to contribute to the account at any age.
- With a traditional IRA, you have to begin liquidating the funds by taking at least minimum annual withdrawals at age 70.5; with a Roth IRA, you do not have to begin withdrawing money at age 70.5.
- With a traditional IRA, early withdrawals (before age 59.5) are taxed as ordinary income and incur a 10-percent penalty on the amount withdrawn; with a Roth IRA early withdrawals (before age 59.5, or less than five years after

the account was established) incur a 10 percent penalty and only the gains are taxed.

- With a traditional IRA, upon deposit, you do not pay taxes on contributions; with a Roth IRA, upon deposit, you pay taxes on contributions.
- With a traditional IRA, upon withdrawal after age 59.5, you pay ordinary income taxes on contributions, plus taxes on interest earnings and capital gains; with a Roth IRA, upon withdrawal at age 59.5, you do not pay taxes on the contributions, interest earnings, or capital gains.

Question 227: **Can I convert my traditional IRA to a Roth IRA?**

You can convert a traditional IRA into a Roth IRA if your MAGI for Roth IRA purposes is less than $100,000 and you aren't married, filing a separate return. You would pay full ordinary income taxes on your funds in the year of conversion, but you wouldn't have to pay again when you withdraw after you reach age 59.5. It may be worthwhile to convert to a Roth IRA if you have a year with low earnings or large tax deductions and a relatively small traditional IRA, so you can take advantage of your personal exemptions and deductions. However, the taxes you'll incur are high enough that if your account is substantial, you should consult with a tax professional to see whether conversion of your IRA to a Roth IRA is best for you.

Question 228: **Can I use my Roth IRA to pay for college?**

If you are at least age 59.5 and have had your Roth IRA for at least five years, you can withdraw contribution funds and interest earnings or capital gains tax-free and penalty-free to fund your child's education.

However, if you are not age 59.5, or have not had your Roth IRA for at least five years, you can use your Roth IRA funds for qualified higher education expenses (QHEE), as discussed in Chapter 12, without incurring the early 10 percent withdrawal penalty as long as enough QHEE is paid out of pocket. QHEE can be paid tax and penalty-free using a Roth IRA to the extent that they are not covered by payments from Coverdell ESAs, tax-free parts of scholarships and fellowships, Pell grants, employer-provided educational assistance plans, veterans' educational assistance plans, and any other tax-free payment (other than a gift or inheritance) at any age. Taxes are owed under any circumstance when money is withdrawn before age 59.5 from your Roth IRA.

Question 229: **If my child is still very young, should I open a Roth IRA to save for college?**

If you will be age 59.5 or older when your child attends college or graduate school, saving for your children's education in your Roth IRA might make sense. If you withdraw money at age 59.5 or later and the money is used for qualified college or graduate school expenses—tuition, mandatory fees and equipment, books, and supplies—the withdrawal won't be taxed. You can also withdraw money from your Roth IRA tax-free if you are at least age 59.5 and paying for your own college or graduate school expenses. To qualify for favorable tax treatment, withdrawn money must be used to pay for expenses at a school authorized to disburse financial aid. (See *www.fafsa.ed.gov* for a list of eligible schools.)

Question 230: **What are the disadvantages of using a Roth IRA to pay for college?**

As always, if you withdraw money from your Roth IRA before you reach age 59.5, you'll owe ordinary income taxes on the share of earnings that you withdraw from the account. Basically, Roth IRA contributions are money that is contributed post-taxes so you never owe taxes on the contributions, but if you withdraw any money before age 59.5, or before having the Roth IRA five years, you do owe taxes on the investment gains. However, if the withdrawn amount is spent on qualified educational expenses, the standard 10-percent early withdrawal fee does not apply. The amount of earnings attributable to early Roth IRA withdrawals is taxed at high ordinary income rates, making early Roth IRA withdrawals a bad choice in most cases, even when paying for college expenses.

Question 231: **How do I save for my retirement if I am self-employed?**

If you have a highly profitable business, recent laws have created fantastic retirement fund options that are a real boon for accumulating wealth in your retirement accounts. On the flip side, as a business owner, the total responsibility for securing your retirement falls on your shoulders. Luckily, you have several options that will allow you to deposit more money into your retirement accounts than most. Look into the following:

- HR 10 Plans
- The Savings Incentive Match Plan for Employees (SIMPLE)
- Simplified Employee Pension (SEP) IRA

Chapter 14

MAXIMIZING YOUR TAX ADVANTAGES

BEING A SINGLE parent has its challenges, and most of them leave holes in your pocketbook, but it also has a few well-deserved tax advantages. Without going into IRS-speak, this chapter explains the tax advantages unique to single parents. However, to make sure you are maximizing your dollars, you'll also want to consult a tax advisor or review generic tax laws annually. What you don't want to do is to miss out on tax breaks that can bolster your savings, your retirement plan, or your child's college funds.

Question 232: Are alimony and child support tax-free?

The tax code is complex, but it's not impossible to decipher, especially when you use a tax preparation software package like TurboTax (used by many financial professionals), or rely on a tax preparation professional. Basically, any alimony you receive is taxable. Child support payments you receive are not taxed, nor are they deductible for the person who pays them.

It's important to note that any alimony you receive won't have taxes withheld from the gross amount, so you usually need to have your employer increase your tax withholding or else pay quarterly or annual estimated tax payments to avoid a fine from the IRS at the end of the year. You are required to pay estimated tax payments if the amount of taxes withheld for you during the year is less than either of these two amounts: 90 percent of the tax shown on your current year's tax return, or 100 percent of the tax shown on your prior year's tax return. You can calculate your estimated taxes for the year with IRS Form 1040-ES.

Question 233: **Are legal fees incurred for a divorce tax deductible?**

Although you cannot deduct the legal fees and court costs for actually getting a divorce, you may be able to deduct the cost of legal advice related to taxes or legal fees paid to negotiate alimony. You may also be able to deduct the cost of home appraisal, actuaries, and accountants whom you used to generate income, such as through alimony, or tax advantages. IRS Publication 504, "Divorced or Separated Individuals," provides guidelines.

Question 234: **Should I itemize my expenses or take the standard deduction?**

In general, itemization will save you money if you have large medical and dental expenses, home mortgage interest, casualty and theft losses, job expenses, a small home-based business, or have made large charitable contributions during the year. The IRS publishes Form 1040, "Schedule A & B Instructions," every year to clarify what payments can be included in your itemized deductions.

Question 235: **What are my filing options?**

The tax code has two options for single parents that can lower the taxes you owe. You can file as "head of household" or as "qualifying widow with a dependent child." Both options substantially raise the income bars that put you in higher income tax brackets. In

2006, single filers earning more than $30,651 typically fell in the 25 percent tax bracket. (You'll need to check this annually.) When filing as head of household, a single mother has to earn $41,051, and a qualifying widow with a dependent child has to earn $61,301, before getting higher standard deductions. In 2006, for example, single filers could claim a $5,150 standard deduction; head of household filers could claim $7,550; and a qualifying widow with a dependent child filer could claim $10,300.

Question 236: **How do I qualify as head of household?**

To file as head of household, you must be "supporting" your child on your own, which means you are either unmarried or living apart from your spouse and filing separate tax returns. Child support payments are not considered taxable income; however, a single mother would have to pay more than half of the child's expenses during the year, including child support payments received, which most are. To file as head of household, you and your children must meet the following requirements:

- The child must be your biological, step, foster, or adopted child.
- The child must live with you at least 50 percent of the year. (If she attends school away from home or travels for long periods, but you are still supporting her, she qualifies.)
- The child cannot provide more than half of support (from trust funds, earned income, or inheritances). Check with the IRS if you are unsure about this provision.
- The child must be under the age of nineteen, though there are exceptions: if she is a full-time student under the age of twenty-four; if she is permanently and totally disabled; if she is not claiming herself on a separate tax return.
- You must pay more than half of the cost of maintaining a home for yourself and your child for the year.

If your child doesn't meet all of the above requirements, but she does meet the requirements for the dependent exemption (see Question 240, on the next page), you may still be able to file as head of household. Consult with a tax advisor or review IRS Publication 501, "Exemptions, Standard Deduction, and Filing Information."

Question 237: **How do I qualify as a widow with a dependent child?**

To file as a qualifying widow with a dependent child, your spouse must have died within the past two years or within the past three years ended December 31 of the tax year for which you're filing. Your children must also meet the following requirements:

- You can claim the dependent exemption for your child
- You were entitled to file a joint return with your spouse in the tax year that your spouse died (even if you didn't actually file a joint return that year)
- You did not remarry before the end of that tax year
- You paid more than half of the cost for maintaining a home for yourself and your child for the entire tax year

You can file a joint tax return in the year your spouse dies and then file as "qualifying widow" for the next two years.

Question 238: **What's the difference between tax deductions and tax credits?**

A tax deduction is a reduction in your taxable earned income. If your taxable income is $30,000, you can deduct the $3,300 dependent exemption from that income to reduce your taxable income to $26,700.

A tax credit is a post-tax deduction in the amount of taxes you owe. If you owed $3,500 in taxes, you could use the child tax credit and deduct $1,000 per child from the amount of taxes to be paid, reducing your taxes to $2,500 if you had one child, to $1,500 if you had two, and so on.

A refundable tax credit occurs when you overpaid your taxes throughout the year. You can add the refundable tax credit to the amount you're owed for overpaying taxes for the year. You can even get a refund for your tax credits if you owed no taxes for the year. Hypothetically, if a single mother with one qualifying dependent child files and owes $0 before the credit, she could possibly be refunded $1,000, but the IRS requires a few conditions be met before a refund is granted. Form 8812, "Additional Child Tax Credit," will help you calculate the actual refund and whether you qualify.

Question 239: **What is the Earned Income Tax Credit and how do I qualify?**

The Earned Income Tax Credit (EITC) offers tax credit to financially challenged parents. If your earned income is less than $31,030 with one dependent child, and $35,263 with two children or more, you may qualify. A worksheet for figuring this credit is included in the book of instructions that accompanies the standard 1040 tax forms. The IRS will also calculate it for you, or you can consult with a tax advisor.

Question 240: **What is the dependent exemption?**

Regardless of whether you itemize your deductions, the dependent exemption offered qualified parents the opportunity to claim $3,300 per child in 2006. When you add a new child to your family, you can claim the exemption for that year, even if the child was born or adopted on New Year's Eve. Typically, the parent with whom the child lives for more than 50 percent of the time claims the dependent exemption. If you share joint physical custody, some parents agree to alternate the deduction from year to year.

However, it behooves you to make sure you are not surrendering this tax asset too quickly. After a divorce or separation, fathers generally have higher incomes than mothers. If you didn't negotiate who would take advantage of the dependent exemption at the time of your divorce or separation, it generally makes sense for you to receive the deduction.

Question 241: **How do I qualify for the dependent exemptions?**

To qualify for the dependent exemptions, all of the following requirements for eligibility must be met:

- The child must be your biological, step, foster, or adopted child. But there are exceptions. (Consult a tax advisor or call the IRS to confirm.)
- The child must live with you at least 50 percent of the year. (Other exceptions may exist; call the IRS to confirm eligibility.)
- The child is under the age of nineteen. There are exceptions: if she is a full-time student under the age of twenty-four; if she is permanently and totally disabled; if she is not claiming herself on a separate tax return.
- The child must be a U.S. citizen or a resident of the United States, Canada, or Mexico.
- Your adjusted gross income must be within the limits established by that year's tax code (less than $150,500 in 2006).

The IRS provides free booklets annually that provide eligibility guidelines. You can find them online at *www.irs.gov* or by calling your local IRS office.

Question 242: **What are child tax credits?**

Regardless of whether you itemize your deductions, and regardless of whether you take the dependent exemption, the child tax credit allows qualified parents to subtract a set amount ($1,000 per child through to 2010, slated to fall to $500 thereafter) from their total tax bill.

Even if you are receiving a refund, you may be able to add a portion of the child tax credit to the refund amount, increasing the amount you'll receive from the IRS. To determine your eligibility and compute your amount, see Form 8812, "Additional Child Tax Credit," and the complementary IRS booklet. To increase the benefit, add the amount gained to your child's college fund account.

To qualify for the child tax credit, you must meet all the requirements for the dependent exemption, with two changes: The child must be under the age of seventeen, and your income must be within the limits established by that year's tax code. As your income increases, the exemption decreases proportionately. If your modified adjusted gross income exceeds $75,000 (as of 2006), you are not eligible. To maximize this advantage, make sure to review the annual IRS *Child Tax Credit* booklet, or ask your tax advisor.

Question 243: **Are there additional tax credits for child care and dependent care?**

Yes, if you qualify, you have additional tax credits available. Basically, a child care tax credit allows you to deduct 20 to 35 percent (depending upon your adjusted gross income) of the first $3,000 you spend per dependent child, per year for qualified child care. A dependent care account allows your employer to set aside a certain amount in pretax dollars to be spent on dependent care per year; this amount cannot be greater than your earned income for the year. You can use both credits to reduce your tax bill, but sometimes the greater benefit comes from selecting one over the other. (See dependent care accounts later in this chapter for more information on how these tax breaks compare.) The IRS outlines its requirements in Publication 503, "Child and Dependent Care Expenses."

Question 244: **How do I qualify for dependent care accounts?**

If your income puts you in the 28 percent tax bracket, and your employer offers the option, you may want to opt for a dependent care account in addition to, or in lieu of, the child care tax break. Note that these accounts must be established by an employer and are limited to your earned income. They also involve planning and paperwork, but if you earn enough money, they can be well worth the effort. For instance, if you set aside $2,500 and are in the 25 percent tax bracket, you immediately save $625 in federal taxes. You also pay less in Medicare and Social Security taxes and may pay fewer state and local taxes.

If your employer offers a dependent care account, jump on board, but make sure you understand the basics guidelines.

Question 245: **Are there any health care tax breaks?**

As a single mother, you have basically two options. You can open a flexible health spending account funded by pretax dollars through your employer, or, if your employer doesn't offer comprehensive health coverage, you can open a health savings account using pretax dollars to cover a high deductible or to pay health care expenses. If you make a lot of money, or if you or your children have extreme medical expenses, you may be among those rare people who benefit from medical and dental deductions. Even though health care premiums are probably your highest medical expense, you cannot use health savings accounts or flexible health spending accounts to cover their costs. Here's what you can do.

Question 246: **Do flexible health spending accounts offer a tax advantage?**

Yes! If your employer offers health spending accounts, you can set aside pretax income to cover your out-of-pocket expenses, including deductibles, co-pays, prescriptions, over-the-counter medications, humidifiers, eyeglasses, and so on. Your benefits administrator can provide you with a list of covered expenses.

Question 247: **Do health savings accounts also offer a tax advantage?**

Yes! If you do not have employer-sponsored comprehensive health insurance, or if the only health insurance you have has a high deductible ($2,000 minimum for a family), you can open a health savings account that will offer tax breaks. For more information and to find a bank near you to open an account, go online to *www.hsainsider.com*. You can use checks or withdraw money to pay any expenses, but you will need to keep all receipts.

Question 248: **Are there any additional medical and dental deductions?**

You can only benefit from these deductions when your out-of-pocket medical or dental expenses are greater than 7.5 percent of your adjusted gross income and you itemize your deductions. You can read more about all of your options in IRS Publication 969, "Health Savings Accounts and Other Tax-Favored Plans."

Question 249: **How can I maximize my tax advantages?**

In general, you need to maximize your tax advantages by adopting some—and preferably all—of the following practices:

- Familiarize yourself with basic tax laws and stay current on annual updates.
- In late December, take time to plan your upcoming financial year to gain maximum benefit.
- Double-check all itemized deductions to make sure you aren't missing a legal deduction.

- Hire a professional accountant or tax consultant (such as seasonal firms that specialize in tax preparation) every year, or at least every two to three years, to make sure you are not overpaying taxes.
- Don't overpay.
- Avoid last-minute surprises.
- Keep meticulous records throughout the year.
- Acquire a home equity loan for major purchases, such as a car or home remodeling.
- Pay yourself first!
- Don't report income that is tax exempt, such as gifts (in 2006, up to $12,000 from one person), inheritances (under $2,000,000 until 2008), group life insurance payments deducted/withheld by an employer, and child support payments.

These are just a few of the tips you can use to lower your tax burden, but it is highly advisable to research your particular circumstances and to consult a tax advisor if you have complicated or confusing questions.

Question 250: **What are the top ten ways to improve my finances?**

1. Stop hiding, and own up to your real circumstances. You can't begin to dig out of excessive debt, elevate your earning potential, bulk up your savings, stockpile a retirement plan, or save for your children's education if you don't look your present circumstances straight in the eye.
2. Create a game plan to get your finances in order. Begin by organizing all the materials, charting expenditures and income, creating a system to stay on top of your finances, and coming up with a game plan for paying down debt and increasing savings.
3. Reduce credit card debt and avoid falling back into that black hole. If you vastly reduce your credit card debt and lower the

interest rates on the few you maintain, you'll be well on your way to renewed financial solvency. The trick is to never fool yourself into thinking those habits are acceptable.

4. Become and remain financially conscious. Once you've dug your head out of the sand, you cannot go back to your over-spending ways and delude yourself into thinking it will all "magically" work out.

5. Reduce expendable spending and increase savings. Create a solid budget that will meet all of your basic needs, trim the fat, and bump up your savings quotient, and you will be on the road to financial health.

6. Vastly increase your financial knowledge. When the savings accumulate, it will be time to make investment decisions. Knowledge is power, so arm yourself and get ready to leap into the big time.

7. Create concrete, realistic goals for your future. Now that you're financially conscious, it's time to set realistic goals that you can meet and expand upon. Just remember—success will breed success.

8. Invest in yourself and your future. Taking measured risks in the investment business is the only way to build your capital assets and increase your wealth.

9. Protect your assets and investments. Making smart decisions to properly safeguard your wealth and your children's financial security is a huge part of financial genius.

10. Plan for your children's education. If you want to give your children the opportunity to get a higher education, you need to activate a serious savings plan now.

THE 250 QUESTIONS

Chapter 1

Question 1: What do I do if my husband suddenly dies or files for divorce?

Question 2: How do I make long-term, calculated decisions?

Question 3: What's the best way to get organized?

Question 4: Speaking of averting disaster, how do I hold my ex-husband accountable?

Question 5: How do I track down a deadbeat dad?

Question 6: How do I handle finances if I hook up with a new man?

Question 7: Should we keep our finances separate?

Question 8: Should we find a way to make it official?

Question 9: What if he moves into my house?

Question 10: What about my other assets?

Chapter 2

Question 11: What's the single most important thing I need to do?

Question 12: How do financial goals serve me on a daily basis?

Question 13: What should be my first and single most important goal?

Question 14: How do I create long-term goals?

Question 15: How do I create short-term goals?

Question 16: How do short-term goals differ from tasks?

Question 17: How do I decide which goals take priority?

Question 18: How do I increase my chances of meeting my goals?

Question 19: How often should I review my progress?

Question 20: Why is the frequency of review important?

Chapter 3

Question 21: What is the first thing I need to do to take control of my finances?

Question 22: How detailed do I have to be when tracking expenses?

Question 23: What would a realistic budget look like?

Question 24: How often do I need to review my budget?

Question 25: Once I have a workable budget, what's the next step to financial health?

Question 26: How do I value my assets?

Question 27: How would a worksheet reflecting my net worth look?

Question 28: When should I consult a financial advisor?

Question 29: What should I ask the financial advisor?

Question 30: What would be a reasonable fee range for a financial advisor?

Question 31: How should I prepare to meet with a financial advisor?

Question 32: How do I evaluate a financial advisor?

Question 33: Do I turn over decisions to the financial advisor or trust my own instincts?

Chapter 4

Question 34: What do I need to know about banking?

Question 35: What are the typical account options?

Question 36: What do I need to ask the banking representative?

Question 37: How do automatic bill payments work?

Question 38: What are scheduled transfers?

Question 39: What are overdrafts?

Question 40: What are direct deposits?

Question 41: Once I select an account, what are the most important things I need to do?

Question 42: How do I know if my money is safe?

Question 43: What is short-term liquidity?

Question 44: What is a money market account?

Question 45: When do I need a money market account?

Question 46: Is there a minimum deposit requirement for money market accounts?

Question 47: Are there advantages to having my money in a money market account?

Question 48: What are certificates of deposit (CDs)?

Question 49: Where do I shop for the best rates on CDs?

Question 50: Are there drawbacks to investing in CDs?

Question 51: What are treasury bills (T-bills)?

Question 52: What are the advantages to investing in T-bills?

Question 53: What is mid-term liquidity?

Question 54: What are bonds?

Question 55: What are treasury notes?

Question 56: What are corporate bonds?

Question 57: What are municipal bonds?

Chapter 5

Question 58: Why is it so dangerous to max out my credit cards?

Question 59: How much debt is acceptable?

Question 60: Is there such a thing as a good debt?

Question 61: Can a bad debt become a good debt?

Question 62: Are credit card charges always a bad debt?

Question 63: If they create bad debt, why is it smart to have credit cards?

Question 64: What are the cons to having credit cards?

Question 65: Why is carrying credit card balances so destructive?

Question 66: Even if you rarely use them, can you have too many credit cards?

Question 67: Are department-store credit cards better or worse than regular credit cards?

Question 68: Is it a good idea to transfer balances?

Question 69: How do I tackle credit card debt?

Question 70: Once I have compiled my credit assessment, what do I do next?

Question 71: Will credit card companies negotiate on terms or a payment schedule?

Question 72: How do I decide which credit cards to pay first?

Question 73: Once I pay my credit cards down, should I continue to use them?

Chapter 6

Question 74: What is a credit report?

Question 75: What information is in my credit report?

Question 76: Do I have any rights when it comes to my credit report?

Question 77: What do I do if I find an error?

Question 78: What if the credit agencies don't correct the errors?

Question 79: Should I hire someone else to clean up my credit report?

Question 80: Once an item is removed, is it gone forever?

Question 81: What if problematic items are my debts?

Question 82: Can I still appeal to have items removed?

Question 83: What if they deny my request?

Question 84: Should I settle old accounts?

Question 85: When should I hire a lawyer?

Question 86: What if all my efforts fail?

Question 87: What if I have positive items that I would want to have on my credit report?

Chapter 7

Question 88: What is a FICO score?

Question 89: What determines my FICO score?

Question 90: Does my income have any effect on my FICO score?

Question 91: Do each of the three agencies have the same score?

Question 92: What is a good FICO score?

Question 93: Why is it important to have a high FICO score?

Question 94: How do I find out my FICO score?

Question 95: Why should I order my FICO score?

Question 96: How often should I request my FICO score?

Question 97: How are my FICO scores used?

Question 98: What damages my FICO score?

Question 99: How do I improve my FICO score?

Question 100: When and how do I take drastic measures?

Question 101: What if I need help resolving my debt?

Question 102: If I work with a credit management company, will it affect my FICO score?

Question 103: What do I look for in a credit management agency?

Question 104: If I'm in a pinch, should I take out a loan to pay my credit cards?

Question 105: When should I look for another job?

Chapter 8

Question 106: What is identity theft?

Question 107: How often does identity theft really occur?

Question 108: How does identity theft occur?

Question 109: How do I protect myself from identity theft?

Question 110: What's the most important information that I should safeguard?

Question 111: How do I protect my Social Security number?

Question 112: How can I protect my credit cards?

Question 113: Is it safe to use my ATM card?

Question 114: Is it safe to provide information over the telephone or Internet?

Question 115: How can I detect identity theft?

Question 116: How can I prevent anyone from hacking into my computer?

Question 117: What if my identity has been stolen?

Question 118: When should I call a lawyer?

Chapter 9

Question 119: If I want to budget for wealth, how do I begin?

Question 120: How do I become a smart consumer?

Question 121: Once my spending is under control, what's the next step?

Question 122: Once I have goals, what do I do first?

Question 123: What constitutes realistic savings goals?

Question 124: How do I monitor my progress?

Question 125: How do I grow my savings over time?

Question 126: How can I make my money grow faster while leveraging my risk?

Question 127: If I'm between the ages of twenty and thirty, how should I invest?

Question 128: How do I invest if I'm between the ages of thirty and forty?

Question 129: How do I invest if I'm between the ages of forty and fifty?

Question 130: How do I invest if I'm between the ages of fifty and sixty?

Question 131: How do I invest if I'm less than ten years from retirement?

Question 132: If I inherit a significant amount of cash, how do I handle the sudden influx of money?

Question 133: What are the seven rules for creating wealth?

Chapter 10

Question 134: Are there times when it makes sense to rent rather than buy?

Question 135: What are the drawbacks to renting?

Question 136: What are the positive reasons for home ownership?

Question 137: What are some of the drawbacks to home ownership?

Question 138: Why does it take so long to build equity in my home?

Question 139: Is it smarter to buy a condo instead of a house?

Question 140: What should I avoid when buying a condo?

Question 141: What do I need to consider when buying a home?

Question 142: What's the difference between prequalification and preapproval?

Question 143: How do lenders determine my eligibility to buy a home?

Question 144: Should I shop around to find the lowest interest rate?

Question 145: How do I determine what I can afford?

Question 146: What is the minimum requirement for a down payment?

Question 147: How does one qualify for FHA-insured or VA-insured loans?

Question 148: What is private mortgage insurance?

Question 149: What are my mortgage options?

Question 150: What are points?

Question 151: What is amortization?

Question 152: What are the advantages to using a real estate agent?

Question 153: How do I find a reputable real estate agent?

Question 154: What happens when I'm ready to buy?

Question 155: What are contingencies, and how do they affect a counteroffer?

Question 156: What else do I need to know about buying a house?

Question 157: If I am selling my home, do I need a real estate agent?

Question 158: Should I make any improvements before selling my home?

Question 159: Do I have to be truthful on my "full disclosure" statement?

Question 160: Is it true that I don't have to pay taxes on a huge portion of proceeds?

Question 161: What do I need to know about buying a car?

Question 162: How do I avoid buying a lemon?

Question 163: Is it better to buy or to lease a car?

Chapter 11

Question 164: Why do I need insurance?

Question 165: What are my options when it comes to health and dental insurance?

Question 166: What are flexible spending plans?

Question 167: What are COBRA and HIPAA?

Question 168: What are health savings plans?

Question 169: How can I save money on health insurance?

Question 170: What do I need to know about life insurance?

Question 171: How much life insurance do I need?

Question 172: How long should I carry life insurance?

Question 173: How can I keep costs to a minimum?

Question 174: How can I make sure I safeguard my home?

Question 175: How do I know which numbers cover what's in my car insurance policy?

Question 176: What can I do to keep my car insurance rates low?

Question 177: How do I research insurance options?

Question 178: How do I find a reputable insurance broker?

Question 179: What do I need to do to make sure my children are protected?

Question 180: Even if I don't have many assets, do I need a will?

Question 181: What is a living trust?

Question 182: What do I do if I want to create a will or a living trust?

Question 183: What is a living will?

Question 184: Do I have to legally file my will?

Chapter 12

Question 185: What is the best way to approach paying for college?

Question 186: So how do Coverdell Education Savings Accounts work?

Question 187: What are the advantages and disadvantages of a Coverdell account?

Question 188: How do Section 529 college savings plans work?

Question 189: What's involved in managing a 529 plan?

Question 190: How do 529 prepaid tuition plans work?

Question 191: How can I make sure the plan will still be available when my child is ready?

Question 192: What other options are available?

Question 193: How do custodial accounts work?

Question 194: Will my child have to pay taxes on her custodial account?

Question 195: Wouldn't it be better to opt for tax-advantaged accounts?

Question 196: What about education savings bonds?

Question 197: How do I purchase education savings bonds?

Question 198: Is there a way to circumvent having the bonds negatively affect financial aid?

Question 199: How do education reward programs work?

Question 200: What is the Hope Credit?

Question 201: Would we also be able to claim the Lifetime Learning Credit?

Question 202: How do federal student aid programs work?

Question 203: How do Pell grants work?

Question 204: How do Supplemental Education Opportunity Grants work?

Question 205: How do Stafford loans work?

Question 206: How do PLUS loans work?

Question 207: How do Perkins loans work?

Question 208: How do federal work-study programs work?

Question 209: Are there any other options for funding college?

Chapter 13

Question 210: How can I secure my retirement?

Question 211: How do employer-sponsored defined contribution retirement plans work?

Question 212: What's the difference between 401(k) and 403(b) plans?

Question 213: What are the advantages of 401(k) and 403(b) plans?

Question 214: What are the disadvantages or limitations of 401(k) and 403(b) plans?

Question 215: How do vesting periods work?

Question 216: What's the difference between nonmatching and matching contributions?

Question 217: Is there a maximum amount I can contribute?

Question 218: Is it ever smart to borrow from my 401(k) retirement plan?

Question 219: What are defined benefit plans?

Question 220: What are profit-sharing plans?

Question 221: What are Employee Stock Ownership Plans (ESOPs)?

Question 222: What are individual retirement plans?

Question 223: How much can I contribute to my IRA each year?

Question 224: What are qualifications or restrictions unique to an IRA?

Question 225: What is a Roth IRA?

Question 226: What is the difference between traditional and Roth IRAs?

Question 227: Can I convert my traditional IRA to a Roth IRA?

Question 228: Can I use my Roth IRA to pay for college?

Question 229: If my child is still very young, should I open a Roth IRA to save for college?

Question 230: What are the disadvantages of using a Roth IRA to pay for college?

Question 231: How do I save for my retirement if I am self-employed?

Chapter 14

Question 232: Are alimony and child support tax-free?

Question 233: Are legal fees incurred for a divorce tax deductible?

Question 234: Should I itemize my expenses or take the standard deduction?

Question 235: What are my filing options?

Question 236: How do I qualify as head of household?

Question 237: How do I qualify as a widow with a dependent child?

Question 238: What's the difference between tax deductions and tax credits?

Question 239: What is the Earned Income Tax Credit and how do I qualify?

Question 240: What is the dependent exemption?

Question 241: How do I qualify for the dependent exemptions?

Question 242: What are child tax credits?

Question 243: Are there additional tax credits for child care and dependent care?

Question 244: How do I qualify for dependent care accounts?

Question 245: Are there any health care tax breaks?

Question 246: Do flexible health spending accounts offer a tax advantage?

Question 247: Do health savings accounts also offer a tax advantage?

Question 248: Are there any additional medical and dental deductions?

Question 249: How can I maximize my tax advantages?

Question 250: What are the top ten ways to improve my finances?

Appendix **B**

RESOURCES

BOOKS ABOUT WOMEN AND MONEY

Smart Women Finish Rich: Nine Steps to Achieving Financial Security and Funding Your Dreams, by David Bach

Girl, Make Your Money Grow! A Sister's Guide to Protecting Your Future and Enriching Your Life, by Glinda Bridgforth and Gail Perry-Mason

The Ten Commandments of Financial Happiness: Feel Richer with What You've Got, by Jean Chatzky

Your Money or Your Life: Transforming Your Relationship with Money and Achieving Financial Independence, by Joe Dominguez and Vicki Robin

Making Bread: The Ultimate Financial Guide for Women Who Need Dough, by Gail Harlow and Elizabeth Lewin

The Nine Steps to Financial Freedom: Practical and Spiritual Steps So You Can Stop Worrying, by Suze Orman

The Road to Wealth: Everything You Need to Know in Good and Bad Times, by Suze Orman

Money, A Memoir: Women, Emotions, and Cash, by Liz Perle

The Soul of Money: Transforming Your Relationship with Money and Life, by Lynne Twist

BOOKS AND WEBSITES ON DIVORCE AND REMARRIAGE

Financial Custody, You, Your Money, and Divorce, by Joan Coullahan, CDP, CFP, and Sue van der Linden, CFP

Money with Matrimony: The Unmarried Couple's Guide to Financial Security, by Sheryl Garrett, CFP, and Debra A. Neiman, CFP, MBA

www.divorce-online.com
www.divorce-help.com
www.nolo.com

CREDIT CARD DEBT, FICO SCORES, AND IDENTITY THEFT CREDIT REPORTING BUREAUS

Equifax
P.O. Box 740241
Atlanta, GA 30374-0241
(800) 685-1111
www.equifax.com

Experian

P.O. Box 949

Allen, TX, 75013-0949

(888) 397-3742

www.experian.com

TransUnion

P.O. Box 1000

Chester, PA, 19022

(800) 916-8800

www.tuc.com

COUNSELING AND INFORMATION

National Foundation for Consumer Credit (NFCC)

Provides credit counseling.

(800) 388-2227

www.nfcc.org

National Association of Consumer Advocates (NACA)

A good resource for finding a reputable law firm to handle credit disputes.

www.naca.org

Identity Theft Resource Center
Help with identity theft issues.
(858) 693-7935
www.idtheftcenter.org

Privacy Rights Clearinghouse
Help with identity theft issues.
(619) 298-3396
www.privacyrights.org

Postal Contact
www.usps.gov/websites/depart/inspect

SEC Office of Investor Education and Assistance
450 Fifth Street, NW
Washington, DC 20549-0213
(202) 942-7040
www.sec.gov/complaints.html

Passport Assistance
www.travel.state.gove/passport_services.html

Federal Communications Commission

Consumer Information Bureau

445 12th Street, SW

Washington, DC 20554

www.fcc.gov

(888) CALL-FCC

Tax Fraud Contact

(800) 829-0433 or,

IRA Taxpayer Advocates Office

(877) 777-4778

BOOKS

Debt-Free by Thirty: Practical Advice for the Young, Broke, and Upwardly Mobile, by Jason Anthony and Karl Cluck

Girl, Get Your Money Straight!: A Sister's Guide to Healing Your Bank Account and Funding Your Dreams, by Glinda Bridgforth

Generation Debt: Why Now Is a Terrible Time to Be Young, by Anya Kamenetz

Your Credit Score: How to Fix, Improve, and Protect the Three-Digit Number That Shapes Your Financial Future, by Liz Pulliam Weston

STARTING YOUR OWN BUSINESS
CONTACT INFORMATION

National Association of Commissions for Women
Provides information and assistance.
8630 Fenton St., Suite 934
Silver Spring, MD 20910
(800) 338-9267
www.nacw.org

Center for Women's Business Research
Nonprofit agency that researches issues related to women-owned business.
1411 K Street, NW, Suite 1350
Washington, D.C. 20005-3407
(202) 638-3060
www.nfwbo.org

Small Business Administration (SBA)
1110 Vermont Avenue, NW, Ninth Floor
Washington, D.C. 20005
Provides extensive information on business setup, business plan creation, pricing, finding employees, financing, budgeting, strategic management, and many other topics specific to women-owned business. They frequently offer one-on-one

counseling and can also help you acquire low-interest loans to get started. Their Service Corps of Retired Executives (SCORE) are available for consultation.

www.sba.gov

Office of Women's Business Ownership SBA
409 Third Street SW, Fourth Floor
Washington, D.C. 20416
(202) 205-6673
www.owbo.sba.gov

Publications Services, MS-127, Board of Governors, Federal Reserve System
Will send you a free copy of *A Guide to Business Credit for Women, Minorities, and Small Business.*
Washington D.C. 20551
(202) 452-3245
www.federalreserve.gov

International Franchise Association
1350 New York Avenue, NW, Suite 900
Washington, D.C. 20005-4709
www.franchise.org

Association of Small Business Development Centers

8990 Burke Lake Road

Burke, VA 22015

(703) 764-9850

www.asbdc-us.org

American Women's Economic Development Corp.

71 Vanderbilt Avenue, Suite 320

New York, NY 10169

(212) 692-9100

www.awed.org

BOOKS

101 Best Home-Based Businesses for Women: Everything You Need to Know About Getting Started on the Road to Success, by Priscilla Y. Huff. A great resource for generating ideas and getting some basic tips on starting up.

Business Plans That Work for Your Small Business, Alice H. Magos and Steve Crow. Good resource for seeing exactly how to format a business plan and what needs to be included.

Free Money and Help for Women Entrepreneurs, by Matthew Leske and Marsha Martello. Has federal and state-by-state information on grants, loans, and special programs or resources for entrepreneurs.

Making a Living Without a Job: Winning Ways for Creating Work That You Love, by Barbara J. Winter

Niche and Grow Rich: Practical Ways to Turn Your Ideas into a Business, by Jennifer Basye and Peter Sander

Starting on a Shoestring: Building a Business Without a Bankroll, by Arnold S. Goldstein, Ph.D. Excellent information on the SBA and how to finance on a shoestring.

Small Business Guide: Starting Your Own Business, by Peter Hingston. Very concise and thorough information in lay terms.

SAVING FOR COLLEGE

SEC's 529 plan website
www.sec.gov/investor/pubs/intro529.htm

Savingforcollege.com
Good information about 529 plans and other means to save for college.
www.savingforcollege.com

The Federal Student Aid website

The definitive information about FAFSA applications and federal education loans. The website also lets you sign up for a FAFSA PIN and submit your FAFSA information online.

http://studentaid.ed.gov

BUYING/SELLING A HOME OR CAR

Bankrate.com

A good source for finding current average money market fund rates, CD rates, and checking account rates. The site also has a mortgage payment calculator that will show you how much your mortgage will cost per month, how much of every payment is interest, and how much pays down the principal balance of your loan.

www.bankrate.com

Edmunds.com

A good source for information about buying new and used cars; includes car reviews.

www.edmunds.com

Realtor.com

The National Association of Realtors' Multiple Listing Service search engine allows you to search literally millions of homes for sale.

www.realtor.com

Yahoo!

This portal site's real estate page provides useful real estate information.

http://realestate.yahoo.com

LeaseGuide.com

An online guide to leasing a car.

www.leaseguide.com

The Federal Reserve's Guide to Vehicle Leasing

www.federalreserve gov/pubs/leasing/resource

PROTECTING YOUR ASSETS: INSURANCE AND WILLS

Life insurance calculators

choosetosave.org

tiaa-cref.org

Life insurance websites

www.term4sale.com

www.ameritasdirect.com

www.insure.com

A.M. Best ratings

www.ambest.com

Standard & Poor's ratings

www.insure.com

Insurance quotes

www.accuquote.com

Termquote (800-444-8376)

Quotesmith (800-556-9393)

Wills and Trusts

www.legaldocs.com

Free Consumer's Tool Kit for Health Care Decision-Making

www.abanet.org/aging

www.practicalbioethics.org

CHILD CARE

Au pairs

www.aupairinamerica.com

www.interchange.org

www.exchanges.state.gov

Alliance of Professional Nanny Agencies (APNA)

Screens nanny agencies.

www.theapna.org

International Nanny Association (INA)
Educates nannies and nanny agencies.
www.nanny.org

National Resource Center for Health and Safety
Day care center licensure and information.
www.nrs.uchsc.edu

Parent Savvy: Straight Answers to Your Family's Financial, Legal, and Practical Questions, by Nihara Chodhri, Esq.
An excellent resource for many parenting issues.

TAXES

The Internal Revenue Service
You can find a ton of useful information and download tax forms from the IRS website. You can also call (800) 829-1040 to speak to an IRS representative, or go to your local IRS office (click on "individuals" and then "contact my local office" to find an office near you, and keep in mind that June through February are the best months to go with a list of questions).
www.irs.gov

Regulations for Your State

You can use this site to obtain information about your state's tax breaks.

www.taxes.yahoo.com/stateforms.html

TEACHING YOUR CHILDREN ABOUT MONEY

Mutual Funds for Children

Stein Roe's mutual fund provides quarterly newsletters with puzzles, contests, and articles aimed at educating children about money.

(800) 338-2550

www.younginvestor.com

USAA First Start Growth

(800) 235-8377

Monetta Express

Money-market account and mutual fund investor programs.

(800) 666-3882

American Express IDA New Dimensions

Provides kids, parents, and money program with investor programs and educational materials.

(800) 437-4332

Kids' Money

Provides inventive tips for teaching children about money.

www.kidsmoney.org

RESOURCES FOR FRUGAL LIVING

BOOKS

The Tightwad Gazette, by Amy Dacyczyn

Frugal Living for Dummies: Practical Ideas to Help You Spend Less, Save More, and Live Well, by Deborah Taylor-Hough

The Mom's Guide to Earning and Savings Thousands on the Internet, by Barb Webb and Maureen Heck

WEBSITES

www.frugaliving.com

www.allthingsfrugal.com

www.thefrugalshopper.com

www.miserlymoms.com

www.lowermybills.com

www.mysimon.com

www.dealtime.com

www.ebay.com

www.ubid.com

www.priceline.com

www.travelocity.com

www.cheaptickets.com

Appendix C

ADDITIONAL READING

365 TV-Free Activities You Can Do with Your Child, by Steve and Ruth Bennett

A Girl's Guide to Money, by Laura Brady

The Standard & Poor's Guide to Saving and Investing for College, by David J. Braverman

The Easy Will and Living Will Kit: Three Easy Steps to Complete Your Will, Living Will, and Powers of Attorney, by Joy S. Chambers

Paying for College Without Going Broke, by Kalman A. Chany with Geoff Martz

The Seven Spiritual Laws for Parents: Guiding Your Children to Success and Fulfillment, by Deepak Chopra

Estate Planning Basics: What You Need to Know and Nothing More!, by Denis Clifford

The Women's Wheel of Life: Thirteen Archetypes of Woman at Her Fullest Power, by Elizabeth Davis and Carol Leonard

101 Things Every Kid Should Do Growing Up, by Alecia T. Devantier

Magic Trees of the Mind: How to Nurture Your Child's Intelligence, Creativity, and Healthy Emotions from Birth Through Adolescence, by Marian Diamond, Ph.D., and Janet Hopson

Business Owner's Toolkit (Second Edition) Launching Your First Small Business: Make the Right Decisions During Your First 90 Days, ed. by John L. Duoba and Paul J. Gada, LL.M., MBA

This Is How We Do It: The Working Mothers' Manifesto, by Carol Evans

The 5 Lessons a Millionaire Taught Me About Life and Wealth, by Richard Paul Evans

The Complete Guide to Protecting Your Financial Security When Getting a Divorce, by Alan Feigenbaum, CFP, and Heather Linton, CPA, DFP, DVA, CDFA

Take Yourself to the Top: Success from the Inside Out, by Laura Berman Fortgang

Nice Girls Don't Get Rich: 75 Avoidable Mistakes Women Make with Money, by Lois P. Frankel

The Girl's Guide to Being a Boss (Without Being a Bitch): Valuable Lessons, Smart Suggestions, and True Stories for Succeeding as the Chick-in-Charge, by Caitlin Friedman and Kimberly Yorio

Fifty Simple Things You Can Do to Improve Your Personal Finances: How to Spend Less, Save More, and Make the Most of What You Have, by Ilyce R. Glink

The Complete Idiot's Guide to Managing Your Money, by Robert K. Heady and Christy Heady, with Hugo Ottolenghi

What It Takes: A Modern Woman's Guide to Success in Business, by Amy Henry

Life or Debt, a One-Week Plan for a Lifetime of Financial Freedom, by Stacy Johnson

The Path: Creating Your Own Mission Statement for Work and for Life, by Laurie Beth Jones

The Money Rules: 50 Ways Savvy Women Can Make More, Save More, and Have More!, by Susan Jones

Go It Alone: The Secrets to Building a Successful Business on Your Own, by Bruce Judson

The Complete Guide to Credit Repair, by Bill Kelly Jr.

The Insider's Guide to Buying a New or Used Car, 2nd Edition, by Burke Leon and Stephanie Leon

Smart Women Take Risks: Six Steps for Conquering Your Fears and Making the Leap to Success, by Helene Lerner

Pitch Like a Girl: How a Woman Can Be Herself and Still Succeed, by Ronna Lichtenberg

Getting Divorced Without Ruining Your Life: A Reasoned, Practical Guide to the Legal, Emotional, and Financial Ins and Outs of Negotiating a Divorce Settlement, by Sam Margulies, Ph.D., J.D.

Miserly Moms: Living on One Income in a Two-Income Economy, by Jonni McCoy

Bonnie's Household Budget Book: The Essential Guide for Getting Control of Your Money, by Bonnie Runyan McCullough

The Divorce Organizer and Planner, by Brette McWhorter Sember J.D.

The Energy of Money: A Spiritual Guide to Financial and Personal Fulfillment, by Maria Nemeth, Ph.D.

Surviving Separation and Divorce: A Woman's Guide to Regaining Control, Building Strength and Confidence, and Securing a Financial Future, by Loriann Hoff Oberlin

The Wall Street Journal Complete Personal Finance Guidebook, by Jeff D. Opdyke

Toxic Success: How to Stop Striving and Start Thriving, by Paul Pearsall, Ph.D.

Building Wealth in a Paycheck-to-Paycheck World: Ten Steps to Realizing Your Dream No Matter What You Earn, by Paul Petillo

Success, Advice for Achieving Your Goals from Remarkably Accomplished People, ed. by J. Pincott

Second Acts: Creating the Life You Really Want, Building the Career You Truly Desire, by Stephan M. Pollan and Mark Levine

Smart and Simple Financial Strategies for Busy People, by Jane Bryant Quinn

The Total Money Makeover: A Proven Plan for Financial Fitness, by Dave Ramsey

The Small Business Start-Up Guide: A Surefire Blueprint to Successfully Launch Your Own Business, by Hal Root and Steve Koenig

The 250 Personal Finance Questions Everyone Should Ask, by Peter Sander, MBA

What I Know Now: Letters to My Younger Self, by Ellyn Spragins

Millionaire Women Next Door: The Many Journeys of Successful American Businesswomen, by Thomas J. Stanley, Ph.D.

Secrets of Six-Figure Women: Surprising Strategies to Up Your Earnings and Change Your Life, by Barbara Stanny

The Martha Rules: Ten Essentials for Achieving Success as You Start, Build, or Manage a Business, by Martha Stewart

The Unofficial Guide to Starting a Small Business, by Marcia Layton Turner

All Your Worth: The Ultimate Lifetime Money Plan, by Elizabeth Warren and Amelia Warren Tyagi

The Complete Idiot's Guide to Starting an eBay Business, by Barbara Weltman

Not Poorer: The Newlywed's Financial Survival Guide, by Deborah A. Wilburn

The Woman's Book of Money and Spiritual Vision: Putting Your Spiritual Values into Financial Practice, by Rosemary Williams

Feng Shui: Do's and Taboos for Financial Success, by Angi Ma Wong

INDEX

ABOUT THE AUTHORS

SUSAN REYNOLDS IS a journalist, author, businesswoman, and single mother who handles her own financial affairs, including managing her retirement fund. She is also the author of *Change Your Shoes, Change Your Life*. She lives in Pembroke, MA.

ROBERT A. BEXTON, CFA has been an investment analyst since 1999. Currently, he manages $70 million of clients' assets for Moirai Capital Management. He holds the prestigious Chartered Financial Analyst designation and earned a B.A. in Economics from UC Berkeley. He lives in San Francisco, CA.